KiTCHEN GENiUS

KiTCHEN
GENiUS

SCOTT GIVOT

MQP

To Ingrid Espelid Hovig and Lars Røtterud,
who encouraged me to begin a New Life
and welcomed me at the threshold.

Published by **MQ Publications Limited**
12 The Ivories, 6–8 Northampton Street
London N1 2HY
TEL: 020 7359 2244
FAX: 020 7359 1616
EMAIL: mail@mqpublications.com
WEBSITE: www.mqpublications.com

SERIES EDITOR: **abi rowsell**
DESIGN: **balley design associates**
LINE ILLUSTRATION: **karen hood**
GENIUS CARICATURE: **chris garbutt**

ISBN: 1 84072 284 3

1 3 5 7 9 0 8 6 4 2

Printed in China

contents

introduction 6

fitting out your kitchen 8

keeping it clean 32

simply shopping 48

preparing & cooking food 80

fruit & vegetables 96

meat, poultry & fish 144

bakery & dairy 176

easy solutions 208

index 220

acknowledgments 224

Introduction

Time and again I have recounted the pearls of culinary wisdom passed on to me by family, friends, and acquaintances. It is a rich legacy. From the time I was six, some of my happiest memories have been set in the kitchen. I have relished my time sitting around the table with my family and enjoying the fruits of our collective labor. More so, I have enjoyed every aspect of the kitchen experience . . . from shopping to cooking to cleaning up. And over the years I have found myself in the company of fellow foodies; each of them enriched by their experiences and each of them generously ready to share their treasure trove of accumulated knowledge.

If someone asks me, "Can you make this rock hard avocado ripe within two hours?" my answer is, "No." But I can send the poor soul back to the market with instructions about what to look for. None of us are necessarily born with an instinct for great cooking, but we can all learn from the experiences of professionals who have stepped into the kitchen before us. This book is about figuring out what you want and the best way of getting it. It is chock full of short cuts and tips—straight from the pen of someone who knows—to make your cooking experience more rewarding. Each chapter provides simple recipes that allow you to entertain family and friends in style.

Begin your culinary adventures with just that—a sense of adventure. Whether you are creating a new kitchen, updating the one you have, preparing a special dinner, or simply tending to business as usual, so much of your success depends upon your mindset. It is not always a matter of having no time. It is a matter of *making time*. Indeed, it is what the journey is all about. When that journey demands your passion and spurs your curiosity, you may find yourself in the midst of a new world. Use this book to navigate your way. Be adventurous with your cooking and creative in the kitchen. Adopt new techniques and remember the old. All the principles of technique amount to very little without the motivation of heart and the desire to nurture yourself and those in your sphere of influence.

Currently we are bombarded with so many questions in regard to food safety, dietary health, and nutrition. There are no easy answers. But when the Great Master and Diva of the culinary world, Julia Child was confronted with years of interrogation as to whether one should eat this or that and what quantities thereof, she consistently responded that just about everything is fine—"in moderation." The fact that she is in her 91st year and has so clearly savored a rich and delicious life is testimony to this sensible and profound advice. I have had the great honor of meeting her on occasion and I will never forget the answer to a question I once raised. I was working on an elementary kids' school project and wanted to teach farming origins, diverse cultural traditions, nutrition, and etiquette. After explaining the concept in further detail, I asked her, "Any tips?" "Serve GOOD FOOD!" was her simple response.

I have written this book primarily for those who feel as though they could use a helping hand. I would be absolutely delighted if other "kitchen geniuses" out there also found this collection useful.

I leave you with an old Buddhist saying: "When you walk into the void, you never come out empty handed." With these words ringing in your ears, clear your counters, set out your ingredients, and slip on your apron. I promise you, this is one celebration of food you won't want to miss.

Scott Hunt

fitting out your kitchen

Looking good, longer

When choosing colors, whether it be for the wall, the floor, or the worktops, think about how many sticky fingers will be ruining your trendy aluminum cupboards, or how obvious the mark caused by spilling turmeric or red wine on your clean white linoleum floor will be. Choose surfaces, walls, and splashback tiles that will be easy to clean to keep your kitchen in tip-top condition.

A fresh look

Look at your kitchen with a fresh eye. Perhaps you want to alter or update it. Perhaps you just want or need to work with what you have. Either way, you can implement improvements to make the space work for you and select the tools that will help you realize your ideal conditions. Take into consideration your aspirations and your budget.

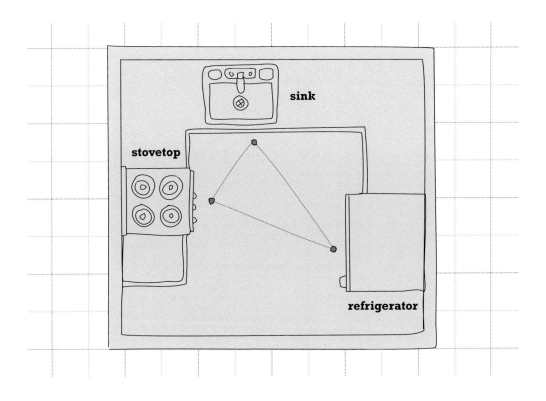

sink

stovetop

refrigerator

A logical working path

Not everyone has the luxury of designing his or her own kitchen. For those that do, consider a logical working path that links the three major elements, refrigerator/ freezer, sink, and stove. They should be near to one another in sequence or form a triangular relationship. The sink, having plumbing considerations, is fixed first. Refrigerated and dry storage for food should be placed as near as possible to the entrance to the kitchen for convenience reasons. Finally, the stove is placed in relationship to the energy sources and in closest proximity to the sink. Counter space may link the three major elements of this "golden triangle," providing efficient transfer and workspace for food and equipment. Minimize the distance between these areas to 20 feet/6 m or less. Create a working path that allows for ease of traffic flow with minimal obstructions.

Fitting the flooring

Think about price and practicality, resilience, a low acoustic level and, above all, the ability to clean with ease. A rubber insulation under the flooring allows you to place an unresilient surface above and still achieve ease in cleaning.

Hardwood flooring

This is hard to beat in terms of aesthetics and sound factors. When well cared for, it improves with age and provides a rich and warm atmosphere. Parquet, plywood, and strip flooring are alternatives if you are considering doing the job yourself. Regular application of a good paste wax will enhance a deep high gloss. An electric polisher will save the knees. Shellac finishes are available for those looking for the easy way out, but do not have quite the same eye appeal.

Linoleum

Linoleum squares or tiles can be laid with ease and are available in a full range of colors and patterns. Should a spot be damaged, it is easy to replace. If the flooring is to be placed over concrete, provide a waterproof underlining. It is recommended to use a damp mop or cloth, followed by dry rubbing for cleaning. Afterwards, simply polish with a quality paste wax for the desired sheen.

Clay quarry, assorted stone, and glazed tiles

These can be beautiful due to the array of colors and patterns available, but can create a colder feeling, both in the appearance and in the temperature of the floor. Consider the cleaning advice for the various materials and note that replacement of damaged tiles will be more challenging.

Limit the damage

Consider the floor of your kitchen if you need casters on large electrical appliances or kitchen units. Casters may damage certain floors; however, they do allow for ease of movement to accommodate cleaning.

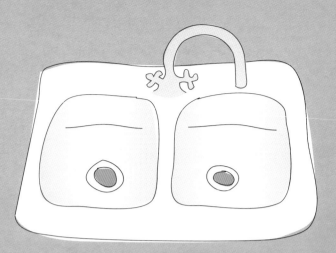

A suitable sink

Enameled, plain aluminum, and stainless steel sinks are currently being replaced by modern treatments of cement and stone. Ultimately your choice should reflect practicality in cleaning, durability, aesthetic appearance, and cost. If space permits, a double sink, which allows for a draining board on either side, is desirable. When there is accommodation for a dishwasher, a single sink with a draining board is sufficient. The sink should have no less than a 10 inch/25 cm depth and a distance of no less than 15 inches/38 cm from the bottom of the spout(s) of the tap to the sink basin. When possible, positioning a sink in front of a window with a pleasant view is desirable, in order to make dish-washing less boring.

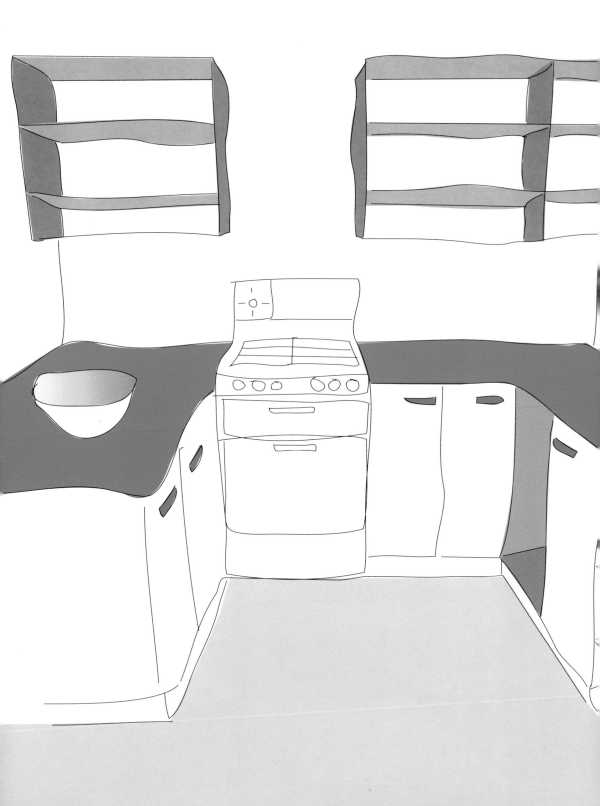

The right cupboard

Instantly improve the look of your cupboards by simply replacing handles or painting worn-out wooden door fronts— you might even consider replacing the doors altogether. Use shelving that is adjustable in height and positioning, and that is accessible without the need for a stepladder. Doors and drawers with rounded corners and recessed handles are good for child safety.

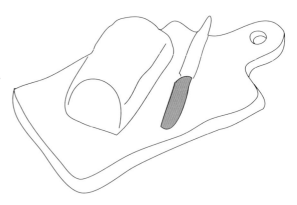

Keeping it clean

Work surfaces should be level, with smooth and clean surfaces. Repair cracks and crevices to avoid collection of food particles and hygiene hazards. Use a commercial kitchen sealant for joins. It is a good idea to have raised or beveled edges on counter working spaces in order to avoid any spills from dripping on to the floor.

Burn-free

Keep steady, heat-resistant tiles or pot stands near the stove in order to protect the work surface from hot pots and pans. Also, so that the pots and pans can be quickly removed from the stove at the end of the cooking process.

Working surfaces

Create work surfaces to the sides and between the refrigerator/freezer, sink, and stove. This will facilitate efficient food preparation, cooking, and washing up when using the appliances.

A room with a view

Install sturdy, treated glass shelves in kitchen windows with undesirable views. This is a good location to grow fresh herbs, particularly during cold seasons. Create a window box on the outside for warmer months.

Cutting it

Increase preparation space by placing a cutting board over the top of the sink cavity. This should fit securely and be used when the water is not running. Many sinks come with a board of this type as an optional extra. If you cannot find one with the right measurements, cut out your own from wood or plastic, with an indentation to one side to allow for easy removal from the sink. Wooden cutting boards are always best because wood contains its own natural enzymes that destroy bacteria.

Storage solutions

Hanging in there

Use wall space under or between cabinets to hang small utensils for cooking preparation. As an alternative to a counter storage block, consider mounting a magnetic plate on the wall to store knives where appropriate. Suspend pots and pans from butcher hooks and frames on the ceiling. Make sure there is ample clearance in height and that the ceiling joists can withstand the weight of your heaviest cookware.

Cool space

Cabinet space that exists on an outside wall of your home is generally cooler. This is where you should store pantry or food products.

Easy-to-clean shelves

Apply a laminated coating to cabinet shelves and drawers. This allows for easy cleaning of grease, dust, and spills. Use uncovered shelving only for the storage of equipment that is used daily, because these areas are prime candidates for dust collection.

Maximize space

Store bread or cutting boards under counters to allow for additional surface preparation space. Everyday appliances, such as the food processor and toaster, may be placed in corners that may otherwise be considered dead space. This makes for easy access when you need them. Keep a flip-top garbage can under the sink for convenience and to prevent the escape of lingering odors.

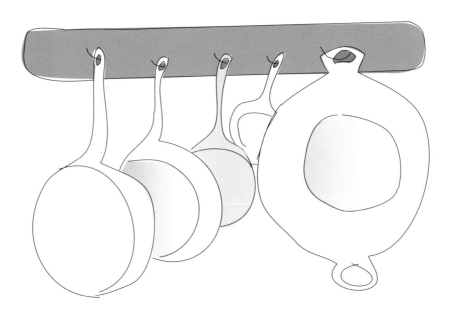

Hidden corners

Use revolving shelves in deep lower cabinets. This is particularly effective for accessibility to corner spaces.

Hot space

Avoid storage space over stoves. It may be dangerous to reach over burners during the cooking process, and the effects of heat, steam, and splattering food creates additional cleaning work.

Lighting

Lighting up

Consider lighting your kitchen for practicality as well as aesthetic reasons. Try to create separate controls to isolate light to the specific areas where you are working. Dimmer switches can optimize the amount of light during the working process. By the same token, you can diminish the intensity of light when the kitchen is at rest and you are entertaining.

Eye level

Store items that you use most often in cupboards located between the height of your knee and your eye level. Pay particular attention to items whose labels can be tricky to read, such as herbs, and keep these as near eye-level as possible. Store items that you seldom use or do not fit elsewhere, such as cake containers or large casserole dishes, in high cupboards.

See what you're doing

Recessed lighting under cabinets and along the ceiling can reduce glare while working. Recessed halogen light bulbs are ideal for this and should be approximately 3 inches/ 8 cm in diameter and roughly 3 feet/90 cm apart. Overhead lighting can create shadow if it is not directly focused, so adjustable halogen spotlights may also be considered to maximize light in particular areas.

Fridge/freezer

The right space

When positioning make sure that the door of your fridge/freezer can be opened fully in the space allowed. If need be, remember that you can re-hinge the door to open from the other side (follow the manufacturer's instructions).

Save energy

Keep your refrigerator out of direct sunlight and away from hot appliances— a five-degree difference in air temperature can have a 20 percent impact on energy consumption. Do not hold the door open unnecessarily, letting out all the cold air. Regularly defrost appliances, if necessary, to keep it in perfect condition.

Easy freezer storage

Clearly label the contents of your freezer so they're easy to find. Divide your freezer into sections—meat, dairy, ready-meals, etc. Choose an upright freezer instead of a chest type as it is easier to organize the contents and find them in a hurry.

Size matters

Rule of thumb has it that if you are selecting a new fridge/freezer, a capacity of 8 cubic feet/0.23 m^2 of fridge for two people should be ample. Add 1 cubic foot/0.028 m^2 for each additional person. For freezer space, 2 cubic feet/0.056 m^2 multiplied by the number of people in your household should suffice for average use. If you are a freezer storage freak, you may wish to increase the capacity Choose a fridge/freezer with adjustable shelves where possible.

Self-defrosting
Save yourself a lot of time and effort and select a fridge/freezer that is self-defrosting.

Deodorizing the refrigerator

Wrap any aromatic food in plastic wrap or seal in airtight containers. If the fridge develops an unpleasant smell, place an open box of baking soda inside to absorb the odor.

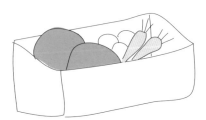

Stove confidence

Consider the height of your stove/oven. Are you confident when lifting pots from the stove, or removing dishes from the oven? You might consider placing the oven at eye level in order to see in directly and avoid bending. In this case, the oven and stove would have to be bought separately, which would mean less economy of space and additional energy source requirements.

Fill the gap

It is quite usual that freestanding appliances, such as a stove or oven, do not fit their allocated space exactly. Therefore, you will often find that a small gap exists between the stove and the worktop to the side of it. This is an ideal breeding ground for bacteria as bits of food can easily fall down the gap. The best way to avoid this is to fill the gap with a made-to-measure piece of surface in a similar style to your kitchen cabinets and worktop, or to buy a piece of plastic specially made for this purpose.

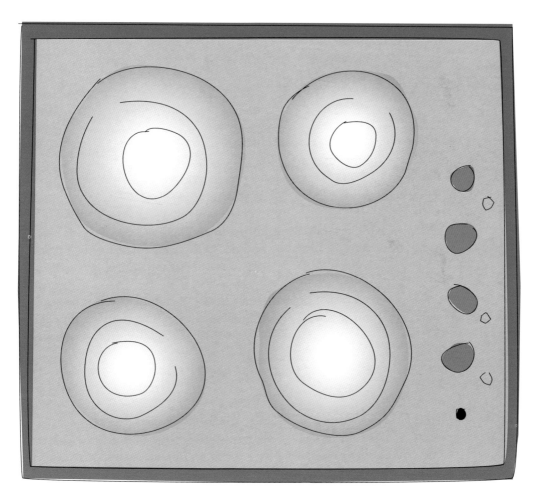

fitting out your kitchen

Additional space

An oven with a strong, well-supported door that pulls down will provide additional surface space for setting pans or casseroles on before transferring to a waist-level countertop. It is very important to have additional workspace provided nearby for easy access.

Size considerations

Think about your capacity requirements when selecting a stove/oven. What size should the oven space be and how many top burners will you need to prepare your largest and most complicated meal? But, remember, don't get carried away—what size can you manage with?

A lot of fresh air

Think about whether you need a fan or ventilation hood above your cooker. This will reduce odors and condensation so is particularly useful in a small kitchen (though there's still the disadvantage of having less space to put it in!). Switch the hood on before you start to cook to create good circulation, and keep it on for a while after you've finished to allow the steam, fat, and fumes to be removed through the pipes and filters to the outside. The more often you cook with fats, the more often you'll have to clean your hood.

Special features

A fan oven helps to ensure an even distribution of heat. A timer acts as a reminder while you are occupied with other activities. Self-cleaning features save time later.

Grilling

Think about a griddle or grilling facility on your stovetop for additional versatility in cooking preparation. Stoves that have a grill feature should also provide space to set prepared food aside and possibly to keep it warm. Some units have a flat cover to place over the griddle or grilling apparatus.

Gas versus electricity

A combination of electric and gas burners has the advantage of economy with the former, and back up in case of power failure with the latter. Gas offers excellent control in regulating heat, and the burners or plates reach the desired temperature rapidly. Some electric burners create an even temperature over longer periods of cooking time; a disadvantage is that these take longer to heat up and cool down, thus increasing the chance of accidents.

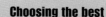

Microwave

Keeping it compact

Choose a microwave that fits your needs, considering the types of food you plan to cook or reheat and quantity. Also, consider the space available. For occasional use, consider a compact model that may fit economically under your kitchen cabinets.

Choosing the best

For quick cooking, select an oven with high wattage. Look for one with self-cleaning wall panels. Digital controls are more precise than manual ones. Microwaves with turntables are preferable for even cooking or defrosting.

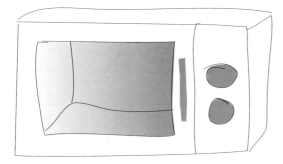

Mixers and processors

Freestanding and hand blenders

Freestanding blenders work independently once adjusted to the desired speed. There is also a pulse mode to give manual control. Because there is a top to the unit, splattering is reduced and contents are confined to the pitcher-like vessel. Use this tool to liquidize, purée, and even emulsify foods and drinks. Add some liquid to solid foods to begin the process. Hand or "wand" blenders are lightweight, take up no space, can be stored easily, and are easy to clean. They can be transferred conveniently for use from a mixing bowl to a casserole dish or cooking pan.

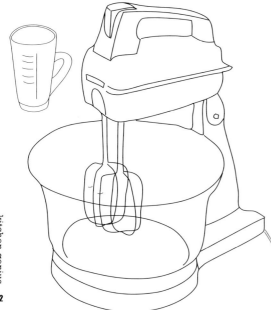

The essential smoothie

Makes 4 glasses

3 cups/660 g mixed berries, kiwi fruit, and/or pineapple
1 banana, peeled

3 cups/750 ml plain yogurt
2 tbsp honey
2 cups/500 ml ice

1 Place all the fruit into the blender and liquidize. Add the yogurt, honey, and ice.

Note: You can add 1 tablespoon of wheat germ before the final blending for additional nutritional value.

2 Pulse until the ice has broken into smaller bits, then blend to a slush-like consistency. Pour into the glasses.

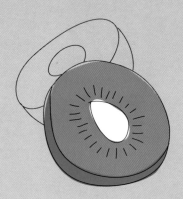

Food processor

A machine that offers great versatility with its blades and tools. These machines make the most labor-intensive of tasks easy and are great for saving storage space because they can do anything from blend to chop to mixing yeast dough. Choose an appliance with a pulse switch to avoid overworking food when you prefer a coarser consistency. A circuit breaker will prevent overheating and burn-out.

Little mixer

A hand-held mixer gives more freedom of movement than standing varieties and is useful if you are short on kitchen space. It's also great for mixing ingredients over heat. Use it for mixing and whisking small quantities of mixture.

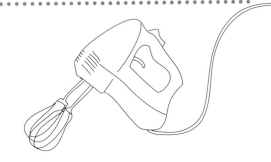

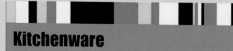

Best place to buy

Restaurant or chefs' supply stores can offer a full line of professional, top-quality kitchen tools. They may not carry the most fashionable names or designs, but their products represent longevity and durability.

Copper

Use copperware for its ability to conduct heat quickly and evenly. Copperware may be used for cooking as well as serving of dishes, such as gratins and casseroles. The best copperware is often lined with nickel or stainless steel, which adds additional weight but true versatility. Avoid using copper when it will come in direct contact with acidic ingredients.

Cast iron

Very heavy and durable, however it needs proper care both prior to and following usage. It commonly comes in the form of Dutch ovens, griddles, and pans, and is perfect for slow-cooking methods, including baking and braising. Cast iron that has an outer layer of enamel may be used for the same equipment, including casserole dishes. Its protective hard surface prevents rusting and it looks smart and decorative when brought to the table.

Aluminum

In general, this cookware is a good conductor of heat and relatively lightweight. Look for aluminum that is coated with nickel, non-stick plastic, or stainless steel to prevent a metallic taste in prepared foods. As long as the coated surface is not damaged, it should not present a health hazard. Remember that exposed aluminum reacts to foods with acid content. If there is no acid in the food, there will be no underlying taste.

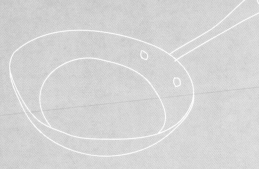

Steel

Steel can be used over or in intense heat and is amazingly durable, although the downside is that it is prone to rusting. Pans, deep-fryers, and woks require proper care and periodic seasoning. Old-fashioned molds and bread pans continue to be designed in tinned steel.

Stainless steel

This cookware withstands acids and often includes has outer layers of aluminum or copper to improve its otherwise inferior ability to conduct heat. An advantage is its non-rusting quality. Stainless steel is found in frying, sautéing, and roasting pans, as well as in saucepans and stockpots.

Nonstick kitchenware

This is often referred to by its brand name, such as "Teflon." It is extremely important to use non-abrasive utensils and cleaning agents with nonstick equipment as the coating can easily be damaged and flaking coating may be toxic when eaten.

Glass cookware

Ovenproof glass cookware has the ability to withstand hot and cold temperatures, so it may be used for cooking, serving, freezing, and reheating, including use in the microwave oven. Consider glass casseroles and baking dishes because while ovenproof glass may not be the best conductor of heat, it holds the temperature well. Flameproof glass may be used on top of the stove on burners.

Roasting pans

Stainless steel roasting pans are probably the best. Heavier ones will not scorch on the bottom when placed on the top of the stove for making sauce. Select one that is rectangular, and with a shape that best fits the contours of your oven. Similarly, make sure the pan is the correct size for the quantities in which you usually cook. The sides should be low enough for heat to access the surface of the food, but deep enough to hold rendered fats and juices. A rack may be placed at the bottom of the pan, allowing for even roasting and for juices and fat to drip away. A pan with handles is also very useful.

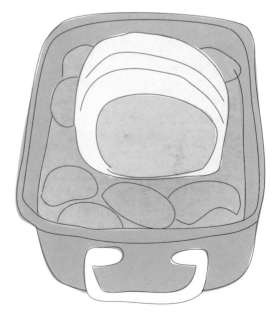

Wooden bowls

These are most suitable for mixing and serving salads. It is best to wipe a wooden bowl clean with a damp cloth. Avoid soap and excess water to prevent warping. Note that use of garlic will impart flavor from its oils to the wood.

Bread pans

The bread pan has sloping sides and is usually aluminum or tinned steel. It comes in a range of sizes, depending on whether you are preparing loaf bread or a rich fortified cake such as fruit bread.

Mixing bowls

Height is important in a bowl for mixing and proving dough. The objective is to prevent drafts, which inhibit the rising process. Glass and ceramic bowls have the weight to sustain balance and stability. Stainless steel bowls have the ability to endure heat and cold. Copper is best for whipping egg whites into a dense texture with maximum volume.: look for a rounded, unlined bottom to achieve the proper angle.

Cake pans

A springform pan is used primarily for cakes that are hard to unmold. Its deep, metal ring is equipped with a spring release clamped onto a removable base, which can easily release the cake. Deep, heavy cake tins are for cakes that need a long cooking time, shallow ones for quick sponges.

Flan dish

A flan dish is usually porcelain, glass, or metal. In the metal version, the outer shallow ring may be separate from the base and is easily removed after baking. Porcelain dishes may be more attractive in appearance, but the pastry base does not cook as well as it does on metal.

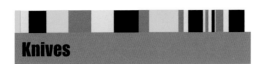
Choosing a knife

Hold a knife before purchase to feel if the grip is balanced and comfortable. The base of the blade should have a firm heel for reinforcement of the blade and as a safety measure. The blade should be riveted and extend through the tang and handle. If you are selecting knives with wooden handles, make sure they are sealed with heat-resistant plastic to avoid any damage whilst cooking. High-quality synthetic or plastic handles are more durable, unlikely to warp, and easy to clean. Above all, always keep your knives sharp for efficiency and safety reasons.

Mezzaluna

The mezzaluna, or mincing knife, has a half-moon shape curvature with single or double blades. There is a handle at either end. It's a great tool for chopping large quantities of herbs and nuts by using a steady rocking motion.

The flashing blade

High-carbon stainless steel is the most practical and expensive choice when selecting knives. It is easy to sharpen and not as prone to discoloration or staining like other compositions.

The cutting edge: four essentials

• A paring knife with a 2 to 4 inch/ 5 to 10 cm length blade is invaluable for peeling and trimming vegetables and fruit.

• Consider a chef's knife for its incredible versatility. The 8-inch/ 20-cm blade size is likely to be the easiest to handle, although the size can vary between 6 to 12 inches/15 to 30 cm. It is large and broad and has the capability to chop, crush, cut, dice, slice, and tenderize.

• Use a filleting knife with a 6-inch/ 15-cm blade to bone fish. It can easily follow the contours where delicate bones must be removed. In addition, it creates fine slices of vegetables and fruit.

• Select a 10-inch/25-cm serrated knife to use for slicing bread and pastry without a tearing effect. A smaller 6-inch/15-cm variety is useful for slicing soft foods with a skin, such as tomatoes and citrus fruit.

Kitchen tools

Scissors

Choose high-quality strong scissors that readily come apart for cleaning. They are great for cutting fresh herbs, dough, pastry, pizza, and poultry. Of course, it is good to also have them handy for opening bags, boxes, and net bags of fruit.

Graters

A four-sided, all-purpose metal grater is the most versatile if you are economizing on space. This should have all the necessary features for slicing and grating in varying degrees of size and texture. If you have enough room, you might consider a nutmeg grater or Parmesan shaver—lovely little tools.

Measuring cups and jugs

Always consider measuring devices that are easy to read. You may wish to consider measurement in metric as well as imperial forms. This allows for adaptability in recipes calling for the system different from yours. Measuring cups and spoons come in plastic, metal, and treated glass to withstand varying temperatures.

Wooden utensils

Collect an assortment of wooden cooking tools. Choose a variety of spoons considering size, length, and bowl capacity (the depth of your cookware). Also add a slotted spoon, spatula, meat mallet, fish slice, and tongs for versatility. Keep them near your stove and use them to protect the finish of your best stainless steel, copper, and non-stick pots and pans.

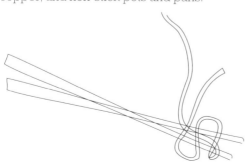

Chopstick magic
Not only are wooden chopsticks good for eating Asian foods, but also for stirring and tossing pasta or noodles during cooking. You won't burn yourself because they do not conduct heat.

Chop chop

Use three cutting boards. Current studies reveal that hard wood is preferred for meat, poultry, and fish. The natural acid in the wood counters health-concerning bacteria. The board should be free of cracks and crevices where food particles may become trapped. Wash in hot soapy water after each use and dry immediately with a clean towel. A second hard wood board should be kept solely for slicing bread. Devote a durable, hard plastic cutting board to the preparation of herbs, fruit, and vegetables.

Thermometer

An "instant read" thermometer is advised for checking poultry and meat doneness. It is preferable to standard thermometers, which are inserted into the flesh from the onset of cooking because the amount of running juices is minimized. The thermometer produces an accurate reading in 2 minutes and may also be used for determining the temperature of liquids and rising dough.

Mortar and pestle

Select a good durable mortar and pestle in heavy stone. It is unlikely to break and there is no possibility of warping. Look for one in an Asian market or kitchen store. It will prove invaluable once you have your dried and fresh herbs sorted out.

Scales

Electronic scales are particularly useful when baking because accuracy is essential. However, good old-fashioned scales often work just as well, albeit more slowly. Do ensure you spend money to make sure that you get an accurate measurement. Antique scales can make a lovely, useful kitchen feature. Don't throw away your old scales if you have some. It might make a nice decoration for your kitchen.

Miscellaneous tools

• Needle-nose pliers are handy for removing fish bones and beards from mussels.

• A melon baller can be used to core apples and pears, remove the seeds from cucumbers, and shape ice cream, sorbets, and chocolate truffles.

• Pasta forks contain a bowled cavity and teeth and help the long-strand pastas to separate during the boiling process as well as when serving.

• Stainless steel ladles in various sizes are useful for serving sauces and soups.

• Elongated metal or wooden tongs are useful for turning sausages while they are being grilled.

• A wide-surfaced fish slice will aid you in filleting and serving whole fish.

• Use natural bristle paintbrushes as pastry brushes or to glaze food for the barbecue. Keep them clean by soaking them in boiling water.

• The best ice cream scoop, whether it has a rounded bowl with spring blade or the flat-shovel model, contains an anti-freezing liquid to prevent sticking.

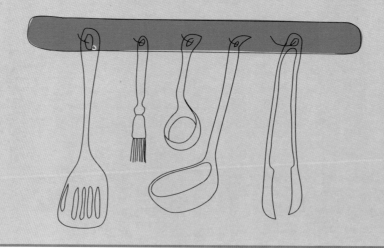

Storage

Roasting bags

These are made of vented, ovenproof plastic. When tightly sealed, they seal in flavors and keep meat moist and juicy.

Plastic wrap

Use plastic wrap to cover anything in the fridge that isn't in a sealed container or bag. It helps to prevent bacteria growth, drying out of food, and arrests lingering odors that might contaminate other foods.

Recycled containers

Choose dry jars that are airtight with screw top lids or flip-tops, preferably uniform in size. Recycle old jars and coffee cans with plastic lids, and use family-sized margarine containers and plastic take-away containers for storing foods in the fridge and freezer. Make sure all recycled containers are thoroughly washed, dried, airtight, and free of rust. Arrange the jars in alphabetical order for quick selection.

Parchment paper

The use of non-stickbaking paper saves greasing baking sheets for cookies and spring form or other pans for cakes. Cut the paper to the size of the pan. The paper lifts off easily and saves cleaning time later. For dishes that require simmering over a long period of time, cut the paper to form a lid over the pan. This allows for a gradual reduction of liquid with the freedom for some air to escape.

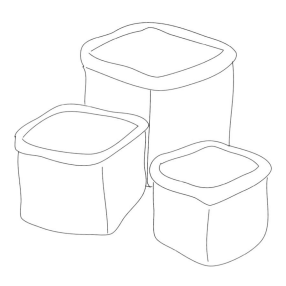

Foiled again

Aluminum foil's pliability makes it easy to mold around cookware and containers, as well as being an excellent conductor of heat. Use it to cover prepared dishes in the oven and line baking sheets. Since food sticks to foil, spray the surface with vegetable oil mist. Line the bottom of your barbecue before pouring in charcoal briquettes. Wrap foods you wish to protect from excessive heat or flame on the grill.

fitting out your kitchen

keeping it clean

The game plan

Tidy up as you go

Remember to clean up and put utensils and ingredients away while you work. This promotes good hygiene, prevents clutter, and saves cleaning up time later.

Sharing chores

Who's going to do the washing up? I learned some rules when I was aged six. Make your life more organized while you cook and have respect and consideration for those who may have to clean up after you (if that's the deal).

Make life easier

Switch your cookware to those with nonstick surfaces. Use a nonstick vegetable oil spray to treat surfaces of hard-to-clean cookware, as well as broilers and barbecues, while they are still cool.

Kitchen telephone

Keep a clean plastic bag near the telephone. If you are using your hands to work with dough or other sticky substances, keep the phone clean by slipping the bag over your hand before you answer.

Easy earthenware

Try pouring water into an unglazed earthenware casserole 1 to 2 hours before usage. By filling both the base and the lid separately, the vessel will be properly treated for use. Not only will this help to create the steam necessary for cooking, but will also reduce excessive absorption of fat from meats, making it easier to clean. Don't use dishwashing detergent for cleaning. Use hot water and a sturdy brush.

Getting the glasses

If two glasses have been stacked and as a result are stuck together, fill the top one with cold water and set the bottom in hot water. Twist them apart gently.

Protect yourself

Many household cleaning agents contain very strong chemicals that could damage your skin. Always make sure you wear protective gloves when you are using them to safeguard your hands, and remember not to rub your face or eyes.

Saving time

Non-rinse cleansers are a quick and easy time-saver when there are only minutes to spare. Wipes that are pre-moistened with detergent will help to speed up the cleaning of kitchen surfaces, handles, and knobs.

Sterilizing jars

Wash clean, and thoroughly rinse jars in which you intend to pot jams, pickles, and preserves. Don't touch the open cavity of the jar and set on a baking sheet in a 250° F/120° C/Gas ½ oven for 30 minutes. This is easier than the rather awkward process of sterilizing jars in boiling water and lifting them with tongs.

Keep on top of it

Wiping up spills and splashes as they happen on your stove will help to avoid having to do major cleaning too often.

Looking after pots and pans

Soaking pots

Pre-soak pots and pans in warm soapy water after usage. Pans or dishes used in preparing foods with egg and dairy products should first be soaked in cold water, followed by washing in hot soapy water. Try to avoid scrubbing as this could damage the surface.

Cleansed corning ware

Clean this cookware by filling it with water and two denture-cleaning tablets. Let stand for 45 minutes. Wash, clean, and dry before usage.

Burnt-on food

When you find that your pan has burnt-on food, fill it with cold water to loosen the grease and charred particles. Change the water several times. Mix a soapy detergent solution into the water and boil it on the stove for 10 minutes. Let it rest, then try scraping the burnt bits off with a non-abrasive bristled brush.

Stain-free stainless steel

This style of cookware should be washed immediately after use if salt has been part of the recipe. This will maintain a smooth surface. Always dry stainless steel after washing to avoid water stains.

Shiny aluminum

Make a solution with the juice of one lemon and water filled to nearly the top of the aluminum pot or pan. Heat to a simmer and the naturally acidic juice of the lemon will remove internal discoloration and stains. When the aluminum begins to look shiny again, remove from the heat, clean, rinse, and dry thoroughly.

Sugar-coated pans

Baking pans or pots that have been used for cooking sugar or sugary foods should be soaked in cold water to breakdown the crystallization.

Teflon soak

Teflon should only be washed with simple hot water and, if necessary, a small amount of detergent. However, remove a difficult stain with a home-made solution. Mix together 1 cup water, 2 tablespoons baking soda, ½ cup bleach, then boil in the stained cookware for 10 minutes, or until the stains disappear. Wash, rinse, dry and condition with a little vegetable oil before using the Teflonware again.

Copper cleaner

Make your own copper cleaner by mixing equal parts of white flour and salt. Add white distilled vinegar and mix thoroughly into a thick paste. Apply with a soft damp cloth to the tarnished spots. Rub gently and let the copperware sit for 10 minutes. Rinse in hot water and immediately dry with a clean cloth. If you own a copper mixing bowl, always scrub it with ½ teaspoon salt and 1 teaspoon distilled white vinegar after use. Wipe it clean with a dry paper towel.

Cast-iron clean-up

After you have used cast-iron cookery equipment, wash it thoroughly clean in soapy water. Choose soap instead of a synthetic detergent. Empty the vessel, dry the bottom, and place it on a low heat until all the moisture inside evaporates. Let it stand to cool. Take a clean paper towel and lightly coat the entire inner surface with a fine layer of vegetable oil to prevent rusting. Try to store this cookware uncovered to avoid undetected moisture and subsequent rust. To treat or season your cast-iron cookware, rub it well with a light vegetable oil and set it in a 250° F/ 120° C/Gas ½ oven for 2 hours. Cool it before usage.

Rust-free chrome

Here's a method for polishing off rust stains. Take a small piece of aluminum foil and wrap it around your index finger. Rub gently over the spot. Take a clean cloth dipped in rubbing alcohol and buff gently. Rub out mildew stains with distilled white vinegar on a clean cloth.

Cleaning appliances

Dishwasher friendly
Freshen your dishwasher by running it on the rinse cycle with ½ cup baking soda.

Easy moving
Kitchen appliances will be more amenable to being moved around for easy cleaning if you rub a little dishwashing liquid in front of their feet before attempting to move them.

Regular cleaning
In general, refrigerators should be cleaned out every two months or so to keep them hygienic and fresh.

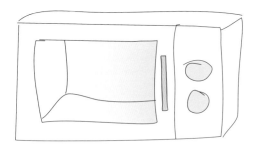

A spotless microwave
If your microwave shows a build-up of food matter, especially at the top, place a bowl of steaming water inside the microwave. Leave it for ten minutes to soften the food deposits, and then wipe the top clean with a damp cloth. A solution of baking soda in warm water will remove odors.

Iron away
The grimy plates on irons can be cleaned when the iron is warm by rubbing with bicarbonate of soda on a damp cloth. Alternatively rub the iron over a damp towel.

Defrosting
Even if your freezer defrosts automatically, an annual cleaning and defrost will keep it in good condition. Be sure to choose a time when your stores in the freezer are low however, as you will need to temporarily remove the contents to insulated bags and boxes.

Cleaning fans and hoods

Avoid a build-up of grease on extractor fans and hoods by cleaning them with a damp cloth rinsed in a hot, weak detergent. Nonelectric, plastic window fans can be unscrewed and soaked in warm, soapy water to remove dust and grease. Use an old toothbrush to clean grime, if necessary, and then rinse and allow to dry.

Perfect seals

Wipe down the rubber seals on dishwashers and washing machines with lemon juice or white vinegar if scale starts to accumulate.

Shiny sinks

On stainless steel sinks you should wash daily with dishwashing liquid. Keep the sink shiny by rubbing with a mix of bicarbonate of soda (or vinegar) and a little warm water.

Porcelain magic

On porcelain sinks try using baking soda, Borax (washing soda) or vinegar to clean thoroughly—if that doesn't work try using a weak solution of bleach left to soak for an hour. Always rinse thoroughly after use.

Too harsh

It is important to avoid using harsh abrasive cleaners and bleach on your sink as much as possible to ensure you keep it looking it's best for longer.

keeping it clean

Chopping board

Stains and lingering smells can be banished from wooden chopping boards by scrubbing with lemon juice and a small clean plastic scrubbing brush.

The family silver

If you have several items of silver or silver-plated cutlery to clean, line the bottom of a plastic bowl with silver foil and place the cutlery on top. Add a handful of washing soda and cover with boiling water: this produces an electrochemical reaction to remove the tarnish. Rinse and dry the cutlery thoroughly.

Tidy toaster

Unplug your toaster before cleaning. Remove bits of stuck food with wooden chopsticks. Shake it gently to allow crumbs to fall to the bottom. Flip the bottom hatch, remove the drawer, or tip it over a sink to discard the loose bits.

Sharp as knives

Steel knives should be hand washed and dried immediately after use to avoid staining and watermarks. If your knife blade is stained, you can gently rub the surface with a wet cork end that has been dipped in a little kitchen cleanser. Wash in soapy water and towel dry immediately. When sharpening knives on a stone, consider using a liquid dishwashing soap instead of a more toxic mineral oil. Soap loosens the steel particles away from the stone. Wash and dry thoroughly following this process.

Bamboo steamer

Never use soap to clean your steamer. Wash it thoroughly with plain hot water.

Rolling pin

Wipe a wooden rolling pin off with a towel and scrape off dried bits with a plastic utensil. Avoid washing the wood to prevent from warping.

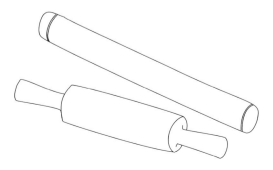

Electric grinder

When you alternate the use of your electric grinder between spices and coffee, always wipe clean with a soft dry towel and gently brush between the crevices. Then grind some dry bread a few times to collect lingering flavors and scents.

Coffee maker

Mineral deposits have a tendency to collect in the filtering system of drip-variety coffee makers. If you use yours daily, clean it on a monthly basis. Fill it with clear water and two tablespoons white distilled vinegar. Brew the solution as you would a pot of coffee. Run this solution through twice, then follow up by running plain cold clear water through twice.

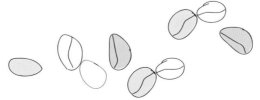

Bubbly blender

Wash your blender pitcher immediately after use. If sticky substances or odors remain, fill it half full with a solution of warm soapy water. Turn on the blender unit to loosen and clean hard-to-reach places on the inside of the container. Rinse clean and dry immediately.

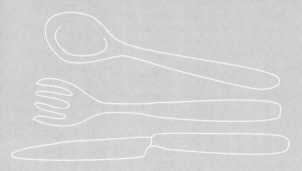

Crystal decanters

Remove some of the white dry scum that forms inside a decanter by filling it with ½ cup distilled white vinegar. Swirl it around and scrub with an elongated brush with an appropriate length handle. Let stand for 20 minutes and repeat the process. Wash with soapy water, rinse thoroughly, and dry.

Hard-to-reach silver

To clean those small, hard-to-reach places or crevices in intricate designs on silver, use an old toothbrush or mascara brush. Use a specialist silver polish or rub in a paste of bicarbonate of soda and rinse off with clean water.

Storage containers

Let's say that your storage containers are clean but have retained a lingering odor. Make a solution of 1 tablespoon baking soda to 4 cups/1 liter hot water. Clean the entire container with a cloth. Rinse thoroughly in fresh water and dry. If the smell of garlic or onion prevails after washing, crumble a clean piece of newspaper into the container and place the lid back on. The odor should be absorbed by the paper and disappear in a few days time. Thoroughly wash the container after discarding the paper.

Cleaning floors

Vinyl flooring

Mop vinyl flooring with warm water and detergent, then rinse with clean water. Any marks that are left can be scrubbed off with emulsion polish.

Slate tiles

A slate-tiled floor should be washed regularly with soap and detergent, then rinsed thoroughly. You can restore the shine on slate tiles by wiping a little milk over the surface.

Easy wood cleaning

Sprinkle damp tea leaves or coffee grounds over wooden floors just before sweeping to help collect the dust. Wipe over unvarnished boards with a damp mop and leave them to dry before polishing with a wax floor polish. Buff varnished boards with a nonslip polish.

Stains and spills

Be sure to wipe up any spillages promptly to avoid staining. Use a suitable cleaner and remember to rinse thoroughly. An abrasive sponge or soft brush can be used to rub away scuff marks using liquid dishwashing detergent and water.

Sturdy flooring

A brick or stone floor should be swept or vacuumed and then washed with warm water and a mild detergent.

Cleaning lino

Marks can be removed from linoleum by scrubbing it with a nonstick scourer and mild detergent or cream cleaner. Use a damp mop and soapy water to clean it thoroughly, and then rinse. If you want a shiny finish, use a special emulsion polish.

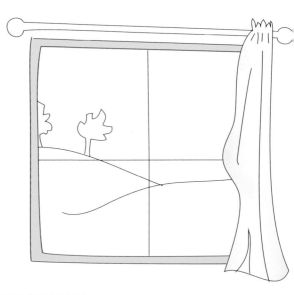

Sparkling glass

The inside window panes usually need washing at least three or four times a year. You should use a mild detergent solution and rinse them with clean warm water. Alternatively, you could make your own window cleaner using vinegar and water in an old plant mister.

Roller blinds

Roller blinds should be vacuumed with the soft brush attachment and, if possible, sponged down with warm water and detergent—you may find that you have to remove them from their fixings to do this. Rinse well with clean water, then leave to dry thoroughly before rerolling.

Venetian or slatted blinds

A useful way of cleaning slatted blinds is to wear cotton gloves that have been slightly dampened and then wipe your fingers along each slat. Always work from the top to the bottom so that dirt doesn't fall on newly cleaned slats.

Curtains

Vacuum curtains regularly with the soft brush attachment working from the top to the bottom. If you need to take the curtains down for cleaning or washing make sure that you mark each inside corner with a permanent marker pen with an R and L for right and left, to remind which curtain goes on which side.

Window frames

Painted and varnished frames should only need an occasional wipe over with a damp cloth wrung out in soapy water. Aluminum frames can be rubbed with a past of Borax (washing soda) and water, then rinsed and polished dry.

Sun isn't always good

Never wash windows on very sunny days because the sun will dry the glass before you have a chance to clean them thoroughly, thus creating smears.

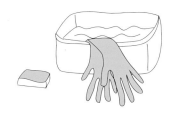

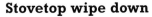

Stovetop wipe down

When flat top burners become encrusted with dried food and splatters, let them cool down after cooking. Once they are cool, cover them with a damp cloth that has been soaked in a grease-cutting dishwashing liquid solution. Wipe clean after 2 hours.

Oven cleaner

Wipe spills and splashes as they happen. Clean racks in soapy water and clean the insides with a branded cleaner. To ensure that any product you use is suitable always read the manufacturer's instructions before you begin. Place a pan of water under the rack of meat or poultry you are broiling to catch any drips and line broiler pans (and even the broiler rack) with aluminum foil. These simple actions will make cleaning much easier.

Refrigerator fresh

Clean inside spillage and stains with light soapy water immediately for safety from contamination and unappealing odors. If odors are apparent, remove all food from the refrigerator and/or freezer and wipe the interior with a solution of 4 cups/1 liter warm water and 1 tablespoon baking soda.

Sink fresh

When juicing and zesting citrus fruits, remember to save any leftover rinds, grind them up, and add them to cold running water in your sink after washing dirty dishes. It will leave a refreshing scent in your sink.

Hot wash

A quick and easy way to clean the oven is to preheat it to its lowest temperature, turn off the power, spray it with a suitable branded oven cleaner, and wipe down with a damp cloth. **Note:** Inhaling chemical products is very bad for health, so read the instructions first and ensure that the area is well ventilated. Check that the cleaner is suitable for use on hot ovens.

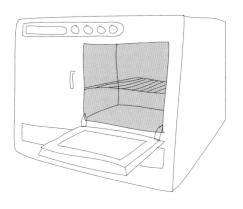

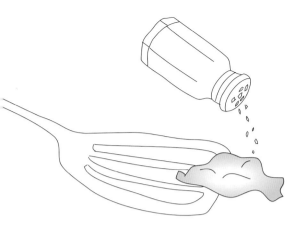

Garbage disposal

When your disposal unit becomes clogged from a build up of fatty substances, fill the cavity with ice cubes and leave to rest for 10 minutes. The fat should coagulate into solid waste. Turn on the disposal and run cold water through.

Sticky-free jars

Whether they are plastic or glass, bottles or jars containing condiments, sweets, or oils should be cleaned after usage. Use a perfectly clean damp cloth to clean the neck threads before the cap or top is replaced. This discourages insect attraction and makes them easier to open the next time.

Oven spots

This technique applies to old-fashioned ovens without self-cleaning capability. Sprinkle salt onto the spot where something has spilled or a casserole dish has bubbled over. Let stand for 10 minutes. Use a metal spatula and scrape the dried food off. Wash with a soapy sponge and damp rinse.

Fabric stains

Remove tomato spots or stains from fabric by pre-soaking fabric in distilled white vinegar. Proceed to wash as usual.

Recycling

If you have a garden and do a fair amount of planting, be environmentally friendly and consider creating a compost heap. Containers are available at most garden and nursery stores. Site the container a considerable distance from your home to discourage the intrusion of animals, insects, and undesirable odors.

All scraps from fruit, vegetables, eggshells, and other organic matter can be transformed into rich humus or fertilizer. Avoid fats and oils, meat scraps, and non-biodegradable substances. Follow instructions as to the frequency of turning the compost matter, and the length of decay time required before use.

Cutlery cleanliness

Place stainless steel cutlery straight into a bowl of soapy water after use to prevent residue from drying between the prongs of forks or staining the metal surface. The same applies to other metals, but avoid soaking cutlery with wood or bone handles— place the ends of these upright in a pitcher of soapy water to keep the handles and their fixings dry.

Keeping germs at bay

Germs love to fester in garbage cans, so emptying the kitchen trash bin daily is essential, whether it is full or not. Wipe the lid daily with an anti-bacterial wipe and clean inside and out weekly with a bleach solution or disinfectant. Always make sure the can is completely dry before putting in a fresh trash liner.

Maintaining marble perfection

Always avoid scratching the surface of marble with abrasive scourers because this can lead to staining. Remove stains by dabbing neat lemon juice or white wine vinegar on the mark and then immediately rinse it thoroughly.

Clean cloths

Make sure that fresh cloths and sponges are used each time you clean to sanitize surfaces, as old materials store bacteria and will recontaminate areas.

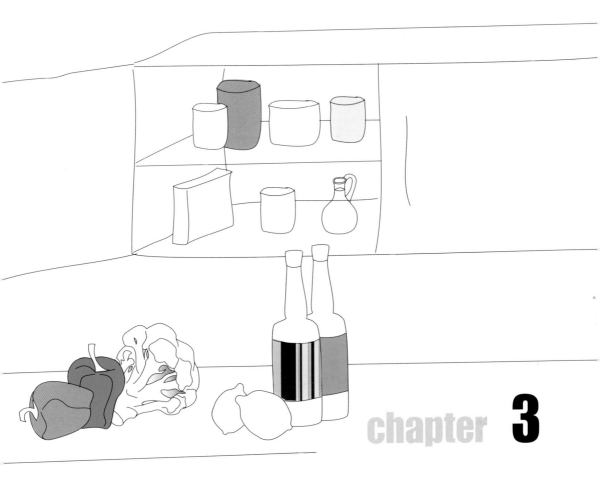

simply
shopping

Planning ahead

Freezing for the future
When planning your meals for the week, consider making quantities that will produce leftovers for freezing or consumption in the near future.

Make a list
Ideally you would shop for fresh foods on a daily basis. Practically speaking, this is not always possible. Depending on how often you shop, plan your meals several days ahead. This way you can check your refrigerator, freezer, and cupboards and organize a list of your needs.

Make a map
Try to organize your list of needs into groups of items as they relate to the layout of the supermarket you shop at, or, if you shop in multiple locations, by what you will purchase in each place.

Aesthetically pleasing
When planning meals, try to visualize how the prepared food will appear on the plate. Consider the contrast in color and the shape of the foods, and aim for textures both smooth and coarse.

Essential supplies
Print and copy a list of the items you need on a weekly basis, leaving spaces free to write in special ingredients. Keep the list on or near the refrigerator to note the items you need as you run out of them.

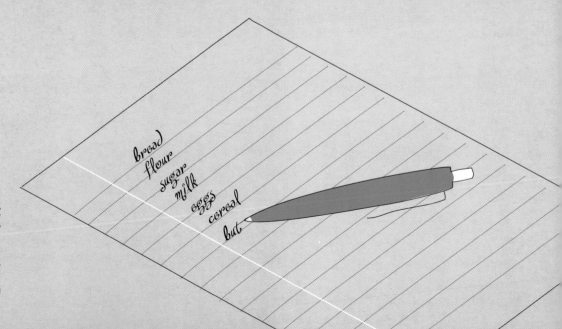

Buy economically

Because of greater availability and lower transportation costs, regional products in season can mean lower prices for the consumer. Check out your local fruit and veg store or market stall before you assume that the supermarket will have the cheapest selection. After a while you'll become accustomed to what is plentiful and then you will be able to plan your meals around this.

Traveling cool

Always select frozen or perishable foods last when shopping at your favorite markets. Create your own cooling transport unit for traveling, especially during hot weather, by lining an insulated bag or basket with frozen ice packs or plastic bags filled with ice cubes.

Get organized

When you go shopping, bring your list and a large metal clip, which you can attach to the shopping cart, allowing for hands-free, easy reference. Reserve a spot to compile all of your clipped coupons in order of expiration date to bring with you on shopping days.

Don't get carried away

Make sure that you buy the essentials—luxury items are lovely, but won't do you any good without the basics.

Buy in season

Farmers' markets can offer the best of what is currently in season and home-grown. These can be situated in city centers or on roadside stands in the country. Consider the choice of buying organic. Seek out the artisan producers of special cheeses, preserved fish, meats, honey, and condiments. In supermarkets consider products that are locally grown. Often these will provide the optimum in flavor and freshness based on seasonality. Consider the same when shopping for fish, meat, and poultry.

simply shopping

Packing

Keep in mind efficiency and safety. Bring a basket or a few sturdy bags along if you will be making multiple stops for single items, or in the event of bag breakage along the way. If you are packing your purchased goods at the checkout, try to keep frozen and chilled items separate from other goods. Pack heavier goods in the bottom of the bags and try to distribute weight evenly on the top. Be careful with delicate and fragile items.

A balanced diet

Always keep in mind that the food you purchase or acquire should be as pure as possible, healthy, balanced, and nutritious.

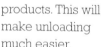

Organization

Pack shopping in bags according to type and how you will store them when you get home: i.e. bags of food for the refrigerator; freezer; dry goods; cans; kitchen cleaners; and bathroom products. This will make unloading much easier.

Can you fit it in?
While you're shopping, consider the amount of space you have to contain your purchases. Overbuying fresh produce will result in wastage if you do not have adequate storage.

Freezing

When freezing foods, label each container with the contents and the date. Store at 0° F/-18° C. A general rule of thumb dictates that you should always use frozen cooked foods within 1 to 2 months. Thaw fish, poultry, and meat in the refrigerator for maximum safety.

Keep it chilled

Generally the coldest zone lies on the bottom shelf of the refrigerator as warm air rises. However the coldest area can be below the freezer compartment when it is positioned at the top of the fridge/freezer. The coldest area should be used for raw fish and meat, prepared dishes, leftovers, cooked meat, and soft cheeses. Frost-free units maintain an even temperature, but always refer to your appliance manual to find the coldest region of your rerigerator.

Safety check

Make sure you check with the grocer as to whether or not certain fresh foods have been frozen before. Fish, meat, and poultry are extra-sensitive foods. It is not advisable to refreeze these items.

Cool zones

Different foods are suited to being stored in different parts of a refrigerator, due to the fluctuations in temperature that arise in various areas. If the coldest refrigerator zone is situated on the top shelf, this is usually reserved for dairy products, non-dairy spreads, cooking fats, and fruit juices. When there is no specific compartment for eggs and butter, they may be stored here as well. Crisper drawers are ideal for unwashed salad items, fruits, and vegetables suited to low-temperature cooling. Shelving on the doors may be used for opened bottles and jars of preserves, condiments, salad dressings, and soft drinks. Vacuum-packed foods are suitable for immediate storage; or you may wish to transfer them into more suitable containers.

Storage considerations

Make sure that you store your foodstuffs safely and efficiently. Correct storage and proper handling of food is essential in maintaining the integrity and nutritional value of raw ingredients for cooking.

Flour

What to choose?

To cover your basic baking needs, buy high-gluten flour for risen bread and low-gluten flour for quick breads, cakes, and cookies. For convenience sake, consider self-rising flour, which is all-purpose flour that includes baking powder. Be advised that this type of flour can deteriorate quickly when exposed to a damp environment.

Can you refrigerate it?

Keep flour sealed in an airtight container and in a cool, dry, and dark place. Refined flour will survive up to 6 months in this condition. If refrigerated, the shelf life is up to a year. Try to use wholegrain flour within a 2-month period in order to maximize the potency of its oily germ. All flour may be frozen for up to 6 months.

Basic white sauce

Makes 2 cups/500 ml

½ **stick/75 g butter**
½ **cup/55 g all-purpose flour**
2 cups/500 ml milk
salt and black pepper

❶ Melt the butter in a deep saucepan. Stir in the flour gradually with a wooden spoon over a gentle heat. Allow the mixture to bubble, but do not cook it so long as to change color.

❷ Remove from the heat and add half the milk. Return to medium heat and stir until the mixture thickens. Beat vigorously for 1 minute. Add the rest of the milk and stir vigorously until it has reached the desired consistency. Sprinkle in salt and pepper to taste.

How to make self-rising flour

Make self-rising flour by combining 4 cups/450 g all-purpose flour with 1 teaspoon salt and 1 tablespoon baking powder. Mix the ingredients well and store in an airtight container. Always sift flour before measuring.

Basic white loaf

4½ cups/500 g white bread flour,
plus extra for dusting
1 tbsp/15 g butter
1 tbsp salt

Makes 1 large loaf
2 tsp/10 ml instant yeast
a scant 2 cups/500 ml lukewarm
water
oil for greasing in an oil mister

① Generously grease a 2-lb/900 g loaf pan. Sift the flour into a large bowl. Rub the butter into the flour until combined. Stir the salt and yeast into the flour.

② Make a well in the center of the flour mixture and pour in the water. Mix to a dough, starting off with a wooden spoon and bringing the dough together with your hands.

③ Turn the dough onto a lightly floured surface. The texture will be very rough and slightly sticky. Begin kneading by folding the dough over itself and giving it a quarter turn.

④ Carry on kneading the dough for about 8–10 minutes until it is very smooth and elastic and no longer sticky. Alternatively, knead the dough in a mixer fitted with a dough hook for 6–8 minutes.

⑤ Lightly grease a large bowl. Form the dough into a neat ball and drop the dough carefully into the bowl. Rub a little oil over the surface of the dough, or use an oil mister and spray lightly. Cover with plastic wrap and leave to rise at room temperature for 1 hour or until doubled in bulk.

⑥ After about an hour, the dough will have risen nearly to the top of the bowl. Remove the plastic wrap and tip the dough onto a lightly floured surface. This will knock the dough back. Knead for an additional 2–3 minutes until smooth again.

⑦ To shape the dough, pat into a large oblong. Fold one end to the center, then fold the other end on top. Drop the dough into the prepared tin, seam-side down. Divide the dough in two if making two small loaves.

⑧ Sprinkle the top of the dough with a dusting of flour, then set the pan or pans aside in an oiled plastic bag until the dough rises to the top of the pan. This will take 30 minutes to 1 hour, depending on the room temperature. Meanwhile, preheat the oven to 450° F/230° C/Gas 8.

⑨ Before baking, make a slash down the length of the dough with a sharp knife. Transfer the loaf or loaves to the preheated oven and bake for 40–45 minutes for the large single loaf and 35–40 minutes for the two smaller loaves. The bread is cooked when it is a rich golden brown and sounds hollow when tapped on the bottom. Remove from the pans and return to the oven to crisp the sides and base, about 5 minutes. Let cool completely before serving.

Yeast

Fresh and dry

There are two basic types of yeast—fresh, which is compressed, and dry, which is fast-acting. When interchanging what is called for in a recipe, ½ oz/15 g dry yeast equals 1 tablespoon fresh.

Keeping it under wraps

Fresh yeast should not be exposed to any temperature changes. Keep it wrapped in the refrigerator for up to 2 weeks. It should last up to 2 months if kept in the freezer. Dry yeast should be stored in a dry cool place. Be sure to check the packaging for the expiration date.

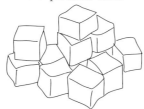

Sugar

Brown versus white

Although in terms of calories, brown sugar is equal to white, it is desirable for its rich flavor and the color and texture it gives to both sweet desserts and savory dishes. It is available in both dark and light forms, with the latter being the softest. The most common brown sugar available is created by combining white sugar and molasses to give it flavor and texture. Demerara sugar is also brown and is in a soft crystal or cube form. Turbinado, or raw palm sugar, is honey-colored and pours in a crystal form. These varieties are primarily used to sweeten beverages.

Keeping it moist

Store brown sugar in an airtight glass container with two wedges of apple to preserve moistness.

Caramel sauce

Serves 4
½ cup/125 g granulated sugar
¼ cup/50 ml light cream

❶ Put the granulated sugar into a small saucepan with 2 tablespoons cold water, and heat gently until dissolved. Bring to the boil and cook for 4–5 minutes until a golden caramel color.

❷ Remove from the heat and stir in the cream. Return to the heat and cook gently, stirring until smooth. Serve with good-quality vanilla ice cream.

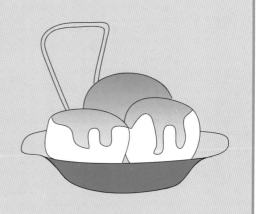

Flakes and crystals

Sea salt and kosher salt are highly favored
in cooking and flavoring because of the
absence of additives and chemicals.
Generally it is in the form of larger flakes
or crystals, so it is advisable to have a
special mill for grinding.

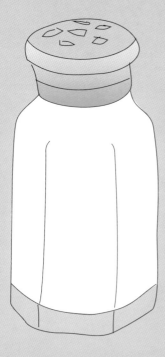

Seasoning with salt

Add a few grains of rice to your saltshaker
to prevent the salt from sticking in humid
climates. Keep a small bowl of coarse salt
near the stove. You'll be less likely to over
season when you use your fingers to
control the amount. Salt will not dissolve in
oil, thus when preparing a salad dressing,
dissolve it first in vinegar or lemon juice.
Then whisk the oil into the mixture.

Grains

Buy in bulk

Whether you are shopping for barley,
bulghur wheat, maize, oatmeal, or wheat,
it is essential to buy it fresh, preferably
from a place where you can buy it in bulk
and are assured of a rapid turnover. The
grain should be dry, plump, and even in
color. The fragrance of a grain is varied
and based on type, but smell for a fresh
grassy aroma, free of must.

Polished or whole?

Refrigerate or freeze whole grains that
you do not plan to use within 5 months,
otherwise store in an airtight container
in a cool, dry place. Polished grains will
keep for up to 1 year in these conditions.
Whole grains, which have the oil germ in
its content, are best refrigerated for up
to 4 months.

Dried beans

Chili fresh

Store dried beans in airtight jars, noting
the purchase date on the lid. It may also
be handy to note the time they may need
to soak and cook for easy reference. By
adding a few dried chilies to the jar, you
can inhibit insect damage during storage.

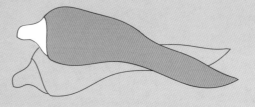

Mexican refried beans

Serves 4–6

2 cups/500 g dried pinto beans
1 onion, finely chopped
3 oz/75 g smoked bacon, chopped
2 dried red chilies, roughly chopped

2 garlic cloves, roughly chopped
1 bay leaf, crumbled
1 tbsp salt
freshly ground black pepper

① Put the pinto beans into a large bowl and pick them over, removing any little stones or beans that are shriveled or discolored. Cover the beans with at least twice their volume of cold water and leave to soak overnight.

② Next day, drain the beans and put into a large saucepan (one that is tall and deep is best as it will reduce evaporation of water). Add the onion, bacon, chilies, garlic, and bay leaf and cover with water by about 3–4 in/7.5- –10 cm (about 6–8 cups/1.5–2 liters).

③ Bring slowly to a boil, skimming off any residue that rises to the surface. When boiling, reduce the heat, cover, and simmer very gently for 2 hours.

④ Add 1 tablespoon salt and continue to cook the beans, uncovered, for another 1 hour or until they are very tender and the liquid is very thick.

⑤ Taste for seasoning and add more salt, if necessary, and black pepper. The dish can be served as it is at this point or you can move on to the next step to make refried beans.

⑥ In a large, nonstick frying pan, heat about 2 tablespoons olive oil. Add 2 cups/500 ml of the Mexican beans you have already made and crush them using a potato masher or fork. Repeat twice more, adding 1 cup/250 ml Mexican beans at a time until the purée is thick and creamy. Serve immediately.

The best beans

When shopping for dried beans, look for uniformity in size for even cooking. The color should be bright and the appearance full. Avoid those that appear cracked or shriveled. Look for expiration dates because the older the bean is, the more it tends to fall apart during the cooking process.

Freezing

Cooked beans can be stored in the fridge for up to 5 days. Freeze cooked beans, covered in their own liquid, in a sealed container for up to 3 months. Use as needed for soups, salads, or side dishes. Alternatively, mash beans into a purée and freeze as a nutritious thickening additive for future soup preparation.

Lentils

Secret ingredients

Preserve color and consistency, and enhance flavor by boiling lentils in water with 1 teaspoon vinegar and 1 sugar cube.

Pasta

Buying the best

The best commercially bought pasta is marked "100 % whole durum" or "pure semolina" and comes from southern Italy. Alternative brands may be inferior in quality and become mushy in the cooking process. Look for a pale golden color. The texture should be rough and an intense wheat flavor imparted. Dry pasta should last indefinitely in a sealed container. Make sure conditions are dry.

Perfect pasta

Always use plenty of water, allowing for a rapid boil before adding the pasta. Long varieties should be grasped at one end and eased into the water at an angle until fully immersed. Never add oil, as this creates a glaze over the surface of the pasta inhibiting absorption of the sauce later. Add 2 tablespoons coarse salt to the water just before you add the pasta. When the noodles are perfectly "al dente" or "to the tooth," meaning that there is a tender texture yet some resistance remaining at the center, the pasta is ready.

Adding sauce

Remember not to overdrain the pasta, retaining a little of the water to loosen it up, and leave it to rest for a few moments. You may preheat your serving bowl and/or plates with the water that you drain from the pot. Empty the water before plating and towel dry. Add a little sauce directly into the pot of drained pasta. Stir for 1 minute on the extinguished burner to allow for the absorption of flavors. Transfer to serving bowls and add more sauce. Toss gingerly before serving.

Bolognese shells

Serves 6

2 tbsp oil
1 onion, finely chopped
1 garlic clove, crushed
2 oz/50 g streaky bacon
1 lb 10 oz/750 g ground beef
3 cups/600 g canned chopped tomatoes

3 tbsp tomato purée (see page 70)
1 tsp mixed dried herbs
1⅔ cups/400 ml milk
1 lb 2 oz/500 g large dried pasta shells
1 tbsp oil
salt and freshly ground black pepper
grated Parmesan, to serve (optional)

❶ Heat the oil in a large saucepan, add the onion and the garlic and cook for 10 minutes. Add the bacon and ground beef and cook over a high heat for 3–4 minutes until the beef has browned.

❷ Stir in the chopped tomatoes, tomato purée, herbs, and 1 cup/250 ml milk. Cover and simmer the bolognese for 40 minutes.

❸ Add the remaining milk and simmer for another 45 minutes.

Taste and season with salt and pepper. Add a little water or stock if the sauce becomes very thick during cooking.

❹ Cook the pasta according to the packet instructions. Drain and toss in the oil. Cool a little, then arrange the shells in a large baking dish. Stuff with the bolognese sauce and bake in a preheated oven, 350° F/180° C/Gas 4, for 15 minutes. Serve with grated Parmesan, if using.

Brown and white rice

Brown rice is generally the choice for those on a health kick. It has a nutty, chewy texture and is probably one of the most nutritious varieties of the grain, since it is not stripped of its outer brown coating. White rice, of which there are many varieties, is probably the most popular. It is stripped of its brown outer covering and used in many main dishes or, more commonly, as a side dish.

The long and short of it

Long-grain rice has a tough starch to dissolve and renders a dry and fluffy texture when cooked. Every grain appears to be separate. Short-grain rice is thicker in texture and has a tendency to stick together. It is used in recipes that call for a wetter and creamier consistency, like risotto or creamy puddings. Short-grain rice sticks together when cooked for a second time making it suitable for dishes such as rice croquettes.

Risotto rice

Forget about rinsing risotto rice so as not to wash away the starch, which is key in the preparation of the dish. You can achieve a creamier-style risotto if you sauté the rice in butter or olive oil first. This creates an initial softening and coating to allow for better absorption later. Thus the starch is released in a gradual manner. If your recipe calls for wine to be used, add it before any additional liquids so that you encourage the absorption of its flavor.

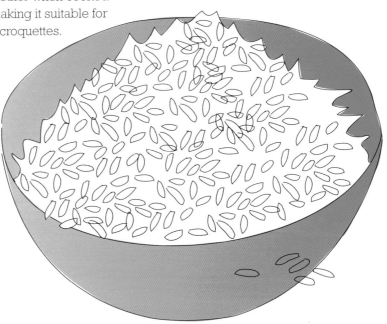

Cooking with your senses

Rinse white rice thoroughly to clean impurities and excess starch. Continue rinsing until the water washes clean. You can rely purely on your senses when cooking rice and forget about measuring the amount of water. Bring a big pot of cold water to a boil. Add a tablespoon of coarse salt. Add a little lemon zest and olive oil as an option. Pour the rice into the boiling water and stir constantly. Test the texture for an "al dente" consistency, then drain off all but a very little amount of water and cover securely with the lid of the pot. Allow to steam for 10 minutes. Fluff with a fork before serving.

Reheating rice

Leftover rice can be reheated in the microwave. Spread the rice evenly over the surface of the largest microwave-safe plate that will fit in the oven. Sprinkle a little water over the top. Cover with a heat-tempered glass top. Set at maximum heat and cook for 3 minutes until piping hot.

Spring vegetable risotto

Serves 6

1 onion	4 cups/1¾ pints chicken broth
1 stick celery	½ cup/125 g fresh peas
2 carrots, peeled	2 medium zucchini
2 tbsp/25 g butter	small bunch mint
1 tbsp olive oil	small bunch parsley
1¾ cups/375 g Arborio rice	Parmesan, to serve

❶ Finely chop the onion, celery, and carrots. Melt the butter with the oil in a large heavy-based saucepan and add the vegetables. Cover and cook, 15 minutes.

❷ Add the rice to the pan and stir well to coat the grains of rice. Pour in about ½ cup/120 ml broth and stir. Cook until the liquid has been absorbed.

❸ Add the same amount of broth and the peas, stir a few times and again leave to let the rice absorb the liquid.

Continue in this way leaving ½ cup/ 120 ml broth in reserve, about 25 minutes.

❹ Finely chop the zucchini and stir into the risotto with the remaining broth. Stir well and season.

❺ Finely chop the mint and parsley with a mezzaluna and mix into the risotto. This dish does not like to hang around so serve immediately with shavings of Parmesan.

The whole thing

Purchase whole seeds and leaves whenever possible for maximum flavor and longevity of shelf life. Buy only a small quantity of your selections at a time. Store herbs and spices in darkness for up to 3 months, or in the freezer for up to 6 months.

Make your own

The taste of the spices in your cooking will be more aromatic and flavorful if you begin with fresh whole spices. Consider a garam masala mix, for example. It can contain up to 12 spices and is primarily added to a dish when the cooking is nearly complete, or sprinkled onto the surface just before serving. Sauté the whole spices in a dry, nonstick pan for 3 minutes. Pulverize them in a grinder and add to your recipe.

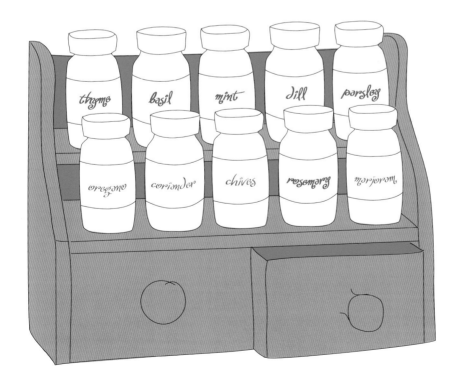

Drying out

To dry fresh herbs, keep the leaves on the stem until they are totally dry. Rub the stems between your fingers and allow the leaves to drop into a spouted vessel. Pour the dried herbs through a paper funnel into your storage container. Retain the stems for flavoring of stocks.

Iced herb tea

4 tbsp fresh herbs, such as peppermint, lemon verbena, or linden blossoms
2 cups/16 fl oz/475 ml boiling water

Makes 2

2 tsp runny honey (optional)
1 lemon, juice only
sprig of mint

❶ Steep the fresh herbs in the boiling water for 10 minutes in a tall pitcher. Strain into another pitcher, add runny honey if sweetness is desired, and cool, then refrigerate for at least 1 hour.

❷ Meanwhile, make ice cubes using lemon juice and fresh mint to avoid watering the beverage down, and add a few cubes to individual glasses for a refreshingly cold beverage.

Icy seeds and nuts

Both seeds and nuts, whether they are shelled or unshelled, store best for longer periods of time if kept in the freezer. Unshelled nuts crack much more easily when frozen and nuts and seeds can be used directly from the freezer.

In the shell

Nuts in the shell should be heavy for their size, even in color, and with no apparent cracks, holes, or blemishes. Avoid any signs of mold or musty smells and make sure that the nut feels hard and is not soft to the touch. Nuts are generally sold in bulk, packaged and ready to eat as a snack, or to use in recipes.

Nut oil

For short-term usage, store both shelled and unshelled nuts in a dark, dry, and cool place in an airtight container. Due to the high content of oil in their composition, nuts begin to turn rancid when exposed to humidity, heat, or light. Nuts retaining their shells survive the longest. Refrigeration prolongs the life of shelled nuts. This also applies for seeds with shells, such as pumpkin or sunflower.

Skinning hazelnuts

Remove the skins from hazelnuts by baking them on a baking sheet in a preheated oven at 325° F/ 170° C/Gas 3 for 25 minutes. While they are still hot, divide them into small groups and wrap in a linen towel. Rub briskly in the towel between your hands. Most of the skin should fall off the flesh. What remains behind will add some color and flavor.

Tasty toasting

Always toast nuts before using them in a recipe as it intensifies their flavor. Heat them in a dry pan until you smell the aroma and look for a light golden brown color in pale nuts, such as almonds and pine nuts. Cool before using in salads. The same principle may be applied to seeds, such as cardamom, coriander, fennel, and star anise. The dry heat releases a pungent aroma and intense flavor. Grind in a spice mill after toasting.

Know your oils

When selecting olive oil, consider the intended usage. "pure" is best for handling high heat temperatures when sautéing. Choose "extra virgin" when it is to be used as a salad dressing or condiment. When buying vegetable oil, check the acid content on the label and select one that has a low content. If you shake the bottle and bubbles appear, they should dissipate fast. This indicates a better quality oil than one with lingering bubbles. Although not the priority in oil selection, choose a bottle with colored rather than clear glass because oil is very light sensitive. General-purpose oils like corn, peanut, and sunflower should have a mild taste and a clear bright color.

How hot?

To gauge the oil's temperature when heating, place a breadcrumb in the frying pan. If the oil is hot enough for frying, the breadcrumb will turn brown and rise to the surface.

How to store

Store all oils in a dark, cool place, and avoid extreme cold as this can often cause the oil to solidify. It will also prevent the oils from going rancid. The shelf life for all oils when properly stored is from 8 months to 1 year.

Chili oil

16 oz/450 g peanut or vegetable oil
2–3 dried piri piri peppers

Makes 1 x 16-oz/450-g bottle
other spices, such as dried coriander, fennel, or five-star anise seed (optional)

❶ Take a sterilized glass bottle or jar with a screw-top lid. Fill it with oil, leaving a small margin of breathing room at the top.

❷ Add 2 to 3 dried piri piri peppers (blazing hot) or another dried variety of your choice. You may also add whole dried coriander, fennel, or five-star anise seed for additional layers of flavor.

❸ Screw on the lid and store in a dry, dark, and cool place with your other oils.

❹ After 2 weeks, fine filter it through a sieve so it is free of any residue. Pour the refined oil into a sterilized and spouted bottle. The oil will extract the flavor of the added ingredients and create extra nuances in the flavor of your dish.

Soy sauce

Dark or light?

Choose the type of sauce that fits your needs. A dark and richer sauce with more viscosity is generally used as a condiment in sauces. The thinner variety, which imparts more sweetness, is primarily used in marinades.

Soy storage

Once a container is opened, it should be refrigerated to maintain potency. Check the expiration date for shelf life.

Soy versus salt

Give recipes a twist by using soy sauce as a substitute for salt when seasoning sauces. It adds both darkened color and enriched flavor. Typically, soy is made from fermented soybeans and has been used as a staple condiment throughout Asia for thousands of years.

Fruity BBQ sauce

Serves 4–6

1 small onion, finely chopped
425-g/15-oz can crushed pineapple or pineapple pieces, drained and finely chopped
2 tbsp cider vinegar
1 tbsp Worcestershire sauce
3 tbsp dark soy sauce

½ cup/125 ml ketchup
1 tsp Dijon mustard
pinch Chinese five-spice powder
1 tsp Tabasco or 1 dried ancho chili, seeded and chopped
1 tbsp molasses
½ lemon, thinly sliced, seeds removed

❶ Put all the ingredients into a medium saucepan and bring to the boil.

❷ Simmer very gently for 1½ hours until the onion and lemon are soft.

Balsamic vinegar

Low-fat flavor

Consider using this as a non-dairy, low-calorie substitute for butter when flavoring cooked vegetables. Create a solution with a little soft brown sugar and use it as the basis for a salt-free glaze to roasted poultry and meat.

Stock

Stock ice cubes

Pour reduced stock into ice-cube trays. Once the stock is frozen, empty into sealed plastic bags. Return the bags to the freezer. Use the cubes for flavoring sauces, poaching vegetables, and cooking savory grains.

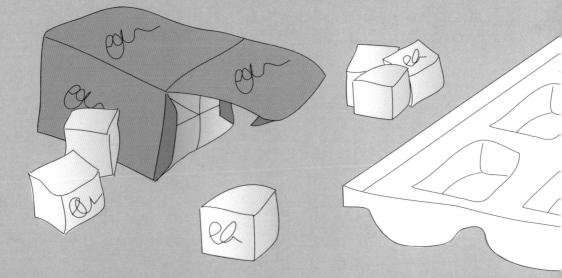

Beef it up

Fortify weak stock with one bouillon cube for every gallon/4.5 liters of liquid. This enhances flavor. It also provides an additional quantity of salt to the stock, so add salt afterwards so as not to overdo it.

Looking after stock

When making fresh stock, always begin with cold water. Cold water brings out the flavors of the ingredients, while hot water seals the flavors in. To remove the thin layer of fat on a pot of stock, simply lay a paper towel over the surface for a moment. Adding an egg white to the stock clarifies it. Stock may also be clarified by running it through a coffee filter. Stock will last a few days in the refrigerator if you don't skim off the fat. This will inhibit bacterial growth. Do not seal the top of the container airtight as the stock needs oxygen to breathe.

Vegetable stock

Keep the excess pulp from vegetables juiced in a juicer. It may be reserved for a low-fat broth or added to stock. It is both nutritious and high in fiber.

Vegetable stock

1 onion	2 garlic cloves
1 leek	10 sprigs of parsley
2 carrots	2 bushy sprigs of thyme
2 celery stalks	5 or 6 peppercorns
1 fennel bulb	1.6 quarts/1.5 liters water
2 tomatoes	2 tbsp tomato purée (page 70)

1 Roughly chop the vegetables. Put them all, together with the herbs and peppercorns, into a large saucepan. Add the cold water and stir.

2 Bring slowly to the boil, then simmer for 40 minutes.

3 Strain and add salt to taste if using as is. Otherwise, don't season but return to a clean pan. Reduce as required, if necessary, before salting.

Cans or tubes?

Keep small cans of tomato purée in your pantry to boost sauces and brown meats, and enrich stews and ragouts. Consider using highly concentrated tomato paste in a tube if you only need small amounts. Its refrigerator shelf life is longer than the can once opened.

Portion control

Left over tomato purée can be frozen in ice-cube trays and used for soups and sauces as needed.

Keeping it fresh

Never store opened tomato purée in a can. Transfer to a sealed plastic or glass container and add a few drops of olive oil before closing.

Homemade tomato purée

3 oz/75 g onions, finely chopped
2 tbsp olive oil
2 tsp all-purpose flour
3 lb/1.5 kg ripe red tomatoes, peeled, seeded, juiced and chopped
⅛ tsp sugar
2 cloves garlic, mashed

Makes about scant 2 cups/¾ pint
1 medium bouquet garni (see page 120)
⅛ tsp fennel
⅛ tsp basil
small pinch coriander
½ tsp salt
1–2 tbsp tomato paste, if necessary
salt and pepper, to taste

① Cook the onions and olive oil slowly together for about 10 minutes, until the onions are tender but not browned.

② Stir in the flour and cook slowly for 3 minutes without browning.

③ Stir in the tomatoes, sugar, garlic, herbs and seasonings. Cover the pan and cook slowly for 10 minutes, so that the tomatoes will render more of their juice. Then uncover and simmer for about 30 minutes, adding spoonfuls of tomato juice or water if the sauce becomes so thick it risks scorching. The purée is done when it tastes thoroughly cooked and is thick enough to form a mass in the spoon. Remove the bouquet garni.

④ If necessary, stir in 1 or 2 tablespoons of tomato paste for colour and simmer for 2 minutes. Correct seasoning. Strain the sauce if you wish. May be refrigerated or deep-frozen.

Pickle juice

Add a little pickle juice to tuna or ham salads. You can also use a little of the juice to flavor sweet and sour dressings in lieu of sugar.

Cut the salt

To eliminate the excess flavor of salt, soak the anchovies in milk for up to 12 hours, depending on the amount of salt you desire. When opening a can of anchovies, do so in a plastic bag to avoid spillage and lingering smells.

Keep it moving

Stubborn flowing ketchup needn't be a problem. Insert a drinking straw into the bottle, push it to the bottom and then remove. Enough air will have been added to begin the flow.

Mustard

Instant salad dressing

When there is a little mustard left in the jar, perhaps a teaspoon or less, add oil, vinegar, seasonings, and honey, if you desire a sweeter taste, to make a salad dressing. Generally the proportions should be 3 tablespoons oil to 1 tablespoon vinegar. Put the lid on the jar and shake sufficiently until all the ingredients are blended.

Olives

A world of olives

Shop for olives best suited to your recipe. They may be found in various preservations of brine, as well as being salt-cured and canned, with or without pits. Buy green olives for braised fish, poultry, and meat dishes; Niçoise for salads and tapenades; and olives stuffed with anchovy, caper, onion, or pimiento as a garnish for drinks, such as a Martini.

Oil, brine, or vinegar?

Store green olives in salted water, herbal brine, oil and/or vinegar in a sealed jar. Preserve black olives in olive oil or brine in a sealed jar or glass container. Olives in oil or vinegar can be stored at room temperature, but canned olives should be refrigerated after opening.

Low-salt olives

When you are using olives for a recipe and they are too salty, first drain the brine. Desalinate the olives by simmering them in water for roughly 10 minutes. Drain and use them as called for. Olives pair well with most meats, particularly lamb and poultry and these low-salt olives retain all of their flavor, without all of the salt.

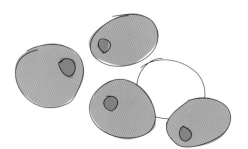

Olive foccacia

Makes 2 loaves

1 tbsp instant yeast
2¾ cups/600 ml lukewarm water
6 cups/700 g white bread flour, plus extra for dusting
1 tbsp salt
1 tsp sugar
1 tbsp olive oil, plus extra for brushing

2 large sprigs fresh rosemary, leaves only, roughly chopped
½ cup/2 oz/50 g pitted mediterranean olives, halved
6 tbsp extra-virgin olive oil
2 tsp coarse sea salt

❶ Whisk together the yeast and the water until the yeast has dissolved. Stir in half the flour until smooth. Cover and set aside in a warm place until the yeast mixture has risen by about one third and is clearly active with lots of bubbles, 1½–2 hours.

❷ Put the remaining flour in the bowl of a mixer fitted with a dough hook and add the yeast mixture, salt, sugar, and olive oil. Mix at the lowest speed until firm but still sticking to the bowl, about 7 minutes. Add more flour or water as necessary.

❸ Increase the speed to high and knead for 1 minute more until the dough is elastic and springs back when pushed with a finger.

❹ Lightly grease a large bowl. Form the dough into a neat ball and drop the dough carefully into the bowl. Rub a little oil over the surface of the dough, or use an oil mister and spray lightly. Cover with plastic wrap and leave to rise at room temperature for 1½–2 hours or until doubled in bulk.

❺ After about 1 hour, the dough will have risen nearly to the top of the bowl. Remove the plastic wrap and tip the dough onto a lightly floured surface. This will knock the dough back. Knead for an additional 2–3 minutes until smooth again.

❻ Turn the dough, which will be sticky, onto a well-floured surface. Flour your hands and tap out into a rough rectangle. Fold in half, then in three in the opposite direction. Divide the dough in two and tap each piece into a rectangle again. Transfer to two floured nonstick 9-x13-x1-inch (23-x33-x2.5-cm) pans, pushing the dough to fill the pans evenly.

❼ Cover both loaves with a dishtowel and leave to rise, about 1 hour. Meanwhile, preheat the oven to 475° F/240° C/Gas 9.

❽ Using the tips of your fingers or the handle of a wooden spoon, poke holes in the dough all over. Sprinkle on the rosemary and olives, then drizzle with the extra-virgin olive oil. Scatter over the coarse salt.

❾ Bake in the center of the oven, 10 minutes. Reduce the heat to 400° F/ 200° C/Gas 6 and cook until golden and risen, 15–20 minutes. Let cool in the pans before serving.

Which chocolate?

Block chocolate with the highest cocoa content will provide the smoothest and richest taste. Sugar content varies from brand to brand, so always test first. Inexpensive brands often have fewer cocoa solids and more sugar.

How to store chocolate

Store in a dark, cool place and away from foods with strong odors, such as onions. Chocolate should be stored moisture-free in freezer paper with an outer layer of foil. Grated chocolate may be frozen, otherwise avoid extreme temperatures for eating chocolate. Frozen chocolate may be measured out into portions for easy usage and is a straightforward way of working with it for sauce and baking purposes.

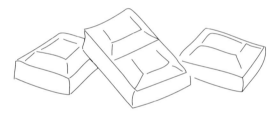

Chocolate curls

Use a swivel potato peeler to shave chocolate as garnish for desserts. Milk and white chocolate curl more effectively than dark due to their softness and pliabile texture.

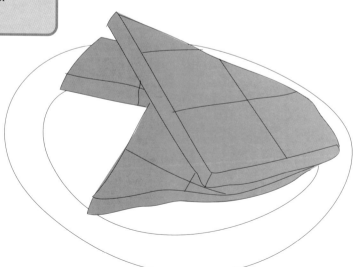

Hot chocolate sauce

Makes 2 cups/450 ml

¾ **cup/115 g semisweet, bittersweet chocolate, chopped**
1¼ **cups/300 ml heavy cream**

❶ Put the chocolate into a heatproof bowl. In a saucepan, bring the cream up to boiling point, remove from the heat and leave for a minute to allow it to come off the boil. Pour the cream over the chocolate. Let stand for about 1 minute, then stir until smooth. Use immediately as needed.

❷ If left to go cold, the chocolate sauce will set. To reheat, put the heatproof bowl over a pan of simmering water. Do not allow the bottom of the bowl to touch the water. Leave the sauce without stirring until melted. Stir to mix and use.

Vanilla beans

Buying beans
Buy vanilla beans that are plump and moist, always avoiding fresh beans that are shriveled.

Vanilla sugar
Partially used fresh vanilla beans may be patted dry with a paper towel and stored in a sealed jar or canister of sugar. The beans should last for future usage and flavor the sugar for special purposes.

Vanilla extract
A drop of vanilla extract in a shellfish soup or sauce will actually bring forth the inherent flavors in the shellfish. Consider this particularly when using sweet shellfish, such as lobster and scallops.

Cold crystals

Store honey in a dark, cool place. Avoid placing it in the refrigerator as it has a tendency to crystallize at cold temperatures, which may produce a grainy texture.

Runny honey
Honey that is hard or crystallized will soften in the microwave. Place a 12-oz/350-g glass jar without its cap in at maximum heat for 45 seconds. This is the perfect way to liquefy honey for cooking.

Sweetness

Honey has a high fructose content, and therefore has a higher sweetening power than sugar. Less honey can be used in place of sugar to achieve the desired sweetness in a recipe. Coat your measuring cup with nonstick cooking spray or vegetable oil before measuring honey and it will slide out easily without sticking.

Baking with honey

Remember to reduce any liquid required in a recipe by ¼ cup/60 ml for each cup of honey used and add ½ teaspoon baking soda for each cup of honey used. Be sure to reduce the oven temperature by 25° F/4° C to prevent over-browning.

The color of honey

The taste and color of honey varies depending on which flowers or herbs grew near the hive. Generally the flavor is milder in the lighter honeys. Pasteurized plain honey is less likely to crystallize over time. Cream or chunky honey has bits of the honeycomb in it, which makes for a good spreading texture.

Coffee

The beans

Whenever possible, buy coffee in the whole, fresh, roasted bean form. Most recipes using coffee as an ingredient will call for intensity. This is achieved by the darker roast varieties. The fresher the grind, the fresher the flavor and aroma will be. Thus, try to grind the beans yourself as needed. Light and heat also diminish taste and aroma, so store in a dry, dark, and cool place.

Coffee and maple syrup frosting

For a cake serving 6–8

¾ cup/175 g butter
scant 1 cup/115 g confectioners'
    sugar
1 tsp instant coffee powder
1 tbsp hot water
4 tbsp maple syrup

1 Beat the butter and sugar together until smooth.

2 Dissolve coffee powder in the hot water, then gradually beat into the frosting with the maple syrup until soft and smooth.

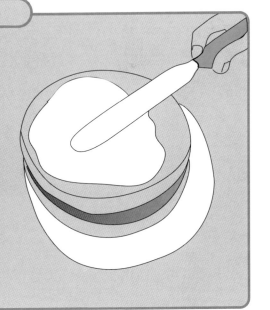

simply shopping

77

Wine in food

Leftover red and white wine can be frozen in ice-cube trays and used as needed for flavoring soups, stews, and sauces.

What to buy?

When shopping for wine, keep a few basic principles in mind. Select wine that you enjoy. Consider wines that can be drunk without food and also wines that can be enjoyed with the food you have prepared. Keep cost in mind and ask for advice from an educated salesperson as to the best value for money. Consider experimenting with new offerings. Allow time for chilling of white and sparkling wines before your meal—2 hours refrigeration time is advisable. Seek advice for opening and/or decanting older vintage white and red wines before your meal. Always buy enough to last the duration of any party.

Champagne

If you don't have a special apparatus for covering leftover champagne, place the handle of a metal spoon down the neck of the bottle. Place in the refrigerator and drink within 2 days. To restore some bubbles to flat champagne, place a raisin at the bottom of the bottle.

Classic champagne cocktail

1 cube sugar
1 tsp brandy
3 dashes Angostura bitters

Makes 1 cocktail
dry champagne, chilled
lemon peel twist, to garnish

❶ Put the cube of sugar into a chilled champagne glass. Sprinkle with the brandy and Angostura bitters.

❷ Pour the champagne into the glass and stir with a glass swizzle stick to mix. Decorate with a twist of lemon peel.

Mineral water

Upside-down bubbles

To retain the bubbles in an opened bottle for as long as possible, store it upside down in the refrigerator.

Water, water, everywhere

Select mineral water from natural springs and look for the lowest sodium content for dietary concerns. Shop for quantity based on consumption. Small, individual bottles are more suitable when only one person is drinking. Mineral water does not maintain its gas for long periods of time after it is opened. Consider recycling factors and money back for containers next time you make your purchase.

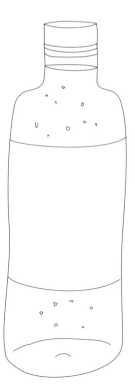

chapter 4

preparing & cooking food

Mise en place

It is vital to prepare food in the correct manner. Having your "mise en place," French for everything in place, and referring to ingredients, prior to cooking, provides you with the confidence and speed to get the work done enjoyably.

Dice

Cut a piece of fruit or vegetable in half and set the flat side down on the cutting board. Cut into slices of the desired thickness. Taking a few of these stacked slices at a time, first cut into strips, then crosswise into diced cube-like shapes. When dicing sticky fruits such as dates, figs, and prunes, keep a glass of hot water nearby to dip your knife in when the sugary residue builds up. Wipe clean with a towel.

Paper plates

Use inexpensive paper plates for organizing preparations with multiple dry ingredients. Lay them out in order of use. The flexibility of the plate also provides control for gradual integration of the ingredients into the mixture by rolling the ends to pour.

Chop

Chop herbs and vegetables finely by beginning with precut small pieces. Assemble the pieces in a small mound. Using the tip of the knife as a pivot, point it at the edge of the mound farthest way from you. Begin to rock the knife, fanning back and forth through the pile. Scrape the pile back into a mound periodically and repeat the process until the ingredient is uniformly chopped. Consider acquiring a double-bladed mezzaluna, which chops with ease using a rocking motion.

Confetti

Coarsely grate vegetables like carrots, celery root, fennel, peppers, rutabaga, and zucchini. Steam or stir-fry until tender for a colorful treat.

Chiffonade

To cut leafy herbs or vegetables, stack the desired quantity of leaves uniformly, one on top of the other. From the stem or widest end, tightly jelly roll them into a cylinder shape. Cut into thin slices for an even, finely shredded look, known as a chiffonade. As an example, select 4 leaves of romaine, kale, sorrel, or spinach and 6 leaves of basil or sage for cooking, salad, or garnish preparations.

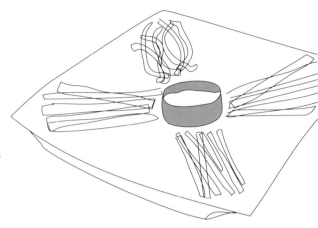

Shredded leaves

Create strips of greens for salads and cooked dishes by first separating leaves. Lay a few leaves of a cabbage, kale, radicchio, or spinach on top of one another. Roll firmly together from the base of the leaf up into a jelly roll shape. Slice the rolls into the desired width strips.

Julienne strips

Raw and cooked julienne vegetables make a terrific garnish for salads, stews, and prepared meat and poultry dishes. Begin by peeling and cutting root vegetables, such as carrot, rutabaga, and turnips, into uniform rectangular blocks. To create matchstick strips, begin by using a vegetable peeler to make wide, thin bands the length of the vegetable. Stack them one on top of the other and slice lengthwise as thin as possible. Blanch in boiling water or stock as a garnish for hot dishes.

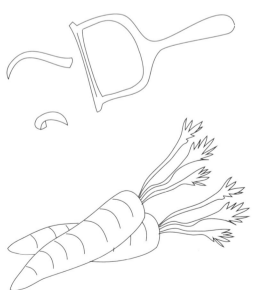

Ribbons

Use a vegetable peeler to slice long, wide strips along the length of carrots, parsnips, and zucchini. Steam or stir-fry the vegetables until tender.

Tenderize

Tougher cuts of meat such as flank steak may call for tenderizing. The intent is to break down the enzymes that make it tough. Score the meat surface with a sharp knife blade in a crosscut fashion. An alternative method, which can also be applied to escalopes of veal, begins with placing the meat between two slices of wax paper. Pound the surface with a mallet or the flat side of a cleaver until a thin medallion is formed.

Slice

Always think safety when slicing fruits and vegetables. Cut whole pieces in half to give one flat side. Place the flat side down on the cutting board and, with your fingertips tucked inward, press firmly to keep it in place. Begin by cutting the part farthest away from you and work towards you. Slice the fruit or vegetable by using your knuckles to guide the knife away from cutting your fingertips. Alternatively, use an egg slicer as a quick and easy time saver to achieve a uniform size when cutting whole, firm mushrooms.

Prevent discoloration

By sprinkling and rubbing your cutting board with lemon juice, you will prevent browning of fruits such as apples, avocados, and pears while dicing. If you are using a number of other ingredients, you may wish to prepare these last, or consider soaking them in water with lemon juice until you are ready to assemble the dish.

Choosing the right equipment

Practice makes perfect

Methods of cooking vary depending on the raw materials at hand and the equipment at your disposal. Select your ingredients and cooking method with the aim of creating tasty, healthy, and nutritious food. As always, practice makes perfect, so don't be afraid to experiment—this way you will educate yourself and learn to execute techniques in a confident and efficient manner.

Oven cooking

When recipes call for a preheated oven, remember to first arrange the internal shelving to accommodate the size of your pans. Set the appointed temperature and heat for at least 10 minutes. Remember that the highest temperature is at the top of the oven and the lower heat is at the bottom. This is particularly important when cooking multiple dishes at the same time. Fan or convection ovens have the advantage of equal distribution of heat throughout, allowing for even cooking at various levels at the same time.

Stovetop cooking

Turn off stovetop electric burners just prior to completion of cooking. There should be enough residual heat to complete the process, and you will save in energy costs.

Microwave cooking

Get to know your microwave thoroughly by fully reading all included instructions. Never use aluminum foil, metal vessels, or other containers with metal detailing because they will severely damage your microwave. When heating foods, remember that it is the outer edge of the dish or container that produces the most heat, whereas the center remains cooler. To ensure even cooking, stir your food or turn the container. Do not put food in the microwave with the power on and leave it unattended—there is a risk of internal fire when a high sugar content exists in food. You can buy microwave shelving, which enables you to cook more than one item at a time.

Leave that door alone

When cooking, avoid opening the oven door needlessly to prevent loss of heat. Every time the door is opened the temperature drops by 25° F/4° C. If your oven door has a window, use it as a visual check for readiness. Always watch the clock or better still, use a timer to track your recipe's cooking progress.

Cooking your food

Boiling

Begin all boiling with cold water, which has a lower mineral content than hot water. Salt water only after it comes to the boil. This will save time in reaching the boiling point. When the pot of cold water has come to a rapid boil, add the vegetables. Cover the pot until the boiling resumes, then remove the lid. Maintain a high boil until the vegetables are cooked "al dente."

Cooking pasta

A lightweight pot is best for cooking pasta. The thinness encourages water to come to the boil faster. Once the pasta has been dropped in, the water will also return to the boil faster. The lesser the variation in temperature while cooking, the better the end product will be.

Draining

Drain the boiled liquid off into a bowl or container to reserve. Add olive oil or butter and seasoning to the vegetables to taste. Quickly place the lid back on the pot and allow 5 minutes to steam. The reserved stock contains vitamins and flavors. This liquid can be refrigerated or frozen and is delicious when used in sauces, soups, or stock.

Blanching

You can blanch soft meats to clean and firm them up. This separates the impurities and proteins from what is salvageable. Likewise, you can blanch bones that are intended for stock. Scum rises to the top, making skimming surfaces easy and aiding in the clarification of stock. Blanching can also be used for reducing strong flavors such as in game or excess salt, as can exist in ham or bacon.

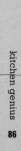

Blanching basics

Blanching helps eggplant lose their bitterness, cabbages diminish in flavor, onions lose their harshness, and tomato skins loosen for easy removal. The time taken for blanching may be as brief as 1 minute for greens and up to 5 minutes for carrots.

Blanching meat

Always begin by setting the meat or bones in a pot of cold water. Bring it to the boil and simmer for up to 10 minutes. Remove any scum that surfaces with a spoon. After the contents are blanched, drain them in a colander and rinse with cold water.

Blanching vegetables

Blanch vegetables in boiling water to precook them for later use. This process draws out the brilliance in color, such as that found in greens, but is useful for freezing excess amounts of vegetables. In the case of root vegetables begin by placing them in cold water in the pan before bringing them to a boil. Others are plunged into the boiling pan.

Poaching

Poaching refers to cooking a food completely covered in liquid, at a temperature just below boiling point. It is best suited to cooking food in advance, as the item being poached will be imbued with moisture. Do not use a lid when poaching as heat becomes trapped and the liquid within could begin to simmer due to the rise in temperature.

Poaching fish

Fish is the main candidate for poaching because wonderful dishes can be created in aromatic juices. Poach whole fish in a court bouillon, comprised of lemon, wine or vinegar, and seasonings. Alternative flavor enhancers include whole peppercorns, bay leaves, ginger, or fennel. Set your fish poacher over two stove burners while poaching large fish. Fish can also be poached in milk to diminish heavy salt or smoke tastes. Always drain the fish on a rack or with towels when you are finished.

Poaching fruit

Keep fruits such as apples, pears, and peaches free from discoloration while poaching by keeping them fully submerged in the liquid they are cooking in. Place a heavy plate over the top of the fruit while they are cooking. This keeps the fruit submerged under the surface of the poaching liquid and allows steam to pass through.

Steamer guide

Steaming is a quick and gentle way of cooking vegetables, and nutrients that seep into water when boiling are retained by this method. It is important to have uniformity in size and density for even cooking. A bamboo or collapsible metal steamer provides the best results. Set the steamer in a wok or pot at least 1 inch/ 2.5 cm above the boiling water. The tenderness of the vegetables should be the same quality as that which is achieved through boiling.

Steamed vegetables

Cut all vegetables into uniform shapes to encourage even cooking. Wrap the vegetables in aluminum foil or parchment paper and place in the steamer. When cooking is completed, pour the nutritious juices over the top or add to a sauce.

Steaming fish

Steaming fish is very similar to poaching it, however, when steaming, a minimum amount of seasoning can be used because it is only diluted by fish juices. The steaming of smaller whole fish, such as sea bass, results in the best flavor.

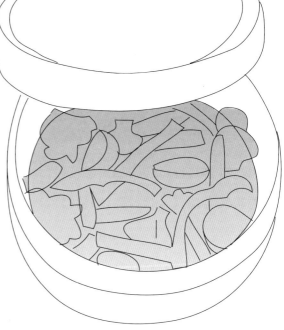

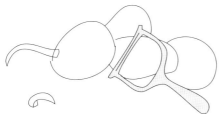

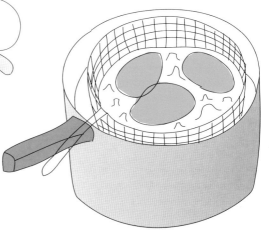

Frying

To keep fat levels to a minimum, use a plastic sandwich bag as a glove for greasing baking pans and casserole dishes with butter or fat. Keep the same glove in a can of vegetable shortening for repeated use. Alternatively, coat a nonstick frying pan with a thin layer of vegetable spray. Never heat the pan for more than 3 minutes before adding the food. When food is to be fried on top of the stove and likely to leave a mess, first cover the top with aluminum foil, leaving only the burners or plates exposed.

Deep-frying

Choose a heavy vessel that allows you to pool oil at least 2 inches/5 cm deep and less than half the height of the cookware. Cast-iron is particularly recommended. Select oil that has a high smoking point. Peanut oil is the best, with canola, corn, safflower, and sunflower oils as the closest alternative. Avoid the low heat tolerance of extra-virgin olive oil. Remember never to deep-fry too much at the same time, as it will lower the temperature considerably. This creates soggy or greasy food. The ideal temperature range is between 325° F–375° F/170° C–190° C. Invest in a fat or sugar thermometer and clip it onto the inside of the vessel for best results.

Electrical deep-fat fryers
If you perform a fair amount of deep-fat frying, you may wish to consider an electrical piece of equipment. It comes equipped with a thermostat so it is easier to adjust the temperature of the fat and maintain an even temperature throughout the frying process. Look for one with safety features including control of splattering and fire prevention.

Tempura vegetables

Serves 4

1 egg
1 cup/250 ml ice-cold water
½ cup/55 g all-purpose flour, sifted
⅓ cup/50 g cornstarch
peanut oil for deep-frying
1 zucchini, thickly sliced
½ small eggplant, cut into strips
1 large red bell pepper, deseeded and
cut into thick strips

2 small red onions, cut into wedges
1 cauliflower, cut into flat slices
2 carrots, cut into thin flat lengths

TO SERVE
4 tbsp Japanese soy sauce
1 scallion, finely chopped
1 red chili, finely chopped
flat leaf parsely

❶ Tempura batter is very light as it uses water rather than milk, and the water must be ice cold. Here it coats a selection of vegetables but it's equally good with raw shrimp, scallops and squid. Serve with a wedge of lemon if you prefer it to the Japanese-style dip.

❷ Whisk the egg and ice-cold water together in a bowl. Sift the flours together then add to the egg mixture and whisk very briefly to combine. The lumps will keep the batter light when it's fried.

❸ Heat the oil for deep-frying to 375° F/190° C/Gas 5. Dip a few pieces of the vegetables into the batter and add to the hot oil. Fry until lightly golden, 2–3 minutes. Remove with a slotted spoon and drain on paper towels. Fry the rest of the vegetables in the same way.

❹ Mix the soy sauce with the scallion and chili and serve in a bowl with the vegetables.

Sautéing

Prevent splattering and burning by tilting a pan of oil or fat away from you when adding ingredients. The liquid pools into a small reservoir on the side farthest away from you. Return the pan slowly to its original flat position. Add salt to vegetables at the same time you begin to sauté for a moist and tender texture. Do not add salt to vegetables if you want them to brown quickly.

Sweating

This method is used for vegetables cooked with a little fat over very low heat. No browning occurs. Sprinkle with a pinch of salt and pepper, and press a piece of parchment paper over the top so that the vegetables are completely covered (paper is better than a lid because air can pass freely and the vegetable surfaces do not dry out). Sweating is often used for soups and stews in order to retain the desired form and texture.

Broiling

Broiling, or grilling, on the stovetop is achieved with a ridged griddle pan. This ridging creates a scoring on the surface of meat, fish, and vegetables. It is essentially equated with pan-frying and is dissimilar to the flavor achieved on the outside broiler or barbecue. It is composed of a cast-iron element and often contains a spout with which the juices can be poured off. A heavy, flat-style griddle with a narrow rim and handle may be used for pancakes and flatbreads.

Electric broiling

The biggest advantage to an electric broiler is that it can reduce cooking times and, if you have a small kitchen where you really need the space, it is also small and easy to tidy away. Choose carefully because some electric broilers will not become hot enough to sear food in the same way that a traditional broiler might.

Stir-frying

In a wok, the surface of the foods should cook quickly and evenly at a high temperature so that the juices are sealed in. Cut each ingredient into uniform shapes for even cooking. Divide the ingredients by cooking time and stage of introduction to the wok, and assemble the plates in order, with the slowest cooking ingredient first and the fastest cooking last. Add barely enough oil to coat or glaze the surface of the wok. When you think the wok is medium to hot, add a small piece of food to the oil before adding the rest, to check that the temperature is right. If the morsel of food pops up, it is ready. Add the food and stir-fry.

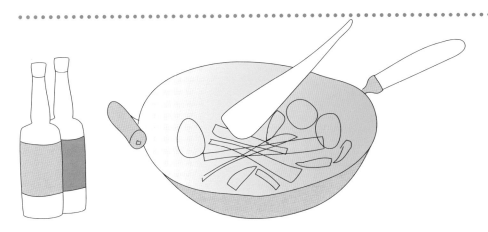

Roasting

Roasting meat means that the food is cooked from all sides in the oven. Roasts with bones retain juices but shrinkage is reduced. Meat is often browned in a little fat or oil on top of the stove first. This seals the surface, adds nice outer color, crisps the fat, and retains juices. Always baste the roast periodically once it is in the oven. This prevents external drying out. Roast meat in a pan that is not so small and compact that the meat steams. This will make the texture tough. By the same token, a pan that is too large will cause the juices to burn. A horizontal rack is commonly used in a roasting pan.

Roasting vegetables

Add onion and large chunks of root vegetables to the roasting pan, such as potatoes, rutabaga, turnip, and carrots, to enhance the flavor of your sauce and accompany your sliced meat on the plate. Roast whole shallots, garlic cloves, and pearl onions in their skins for a treat. Tomatoes added to the preparation of roasts help to tenderize them naturally. They contain acid, which works well to breakdown the enzymes in meat. They also render sweetness. If you are frying meat to seal it before roasting, sprinkle a little paprika over the surface for color and flavor.

Roast beef

Serves 6

1½ lb/675 g fillet of beef
4 medium-sized potatoes
oil, for shallow frying
3 tsp grated fresh horseradish

1 cup/250 g sour cream
1 tbsp chopped fresh chives, plus
  extra to garnish
salt and freshly ground black pepper

❶ Roast the beef in a preheated oven, 220° C/425° F/Gas 7 for 25 minutes. Let cool for 10 minutes.

❷ Meanwhile, thinly slice the potatoes, about 1/16 in/2 mm thick, using the slicing blade of a food processor, discarding the end pieces, which will be too small. (The potatoes shouldn't be quite as thin as a potato fry.)

❸ Heat the oil in large frying pan and cook the potato slices in small batches for 4–5 minutes each side until crisp and golden. Drain on paper towels to remove excess oil.

❹ Mix the horseradish with the sour cream and chives, and season well with salt and pepper. (The dip will thicken up after a few minutes.)

❺ To serve, cut the beef into slices and arrange the slivers of beef on top of some potato slices. Add a spoonful of horseradish cream and garnish with chives.

Chicken rotisserie

Try this technique of setting a whole chicken upright on a vertical rack. This allows for the free circulation of hot oven air all around. Preheat the oven to 450° F/ 230° C/Gas 8. This heat blasts the bird and browns it faster. When browned, reduce the temperature to 375° F/190° C/Gas 5 for the remainder of the cooking time.

The flavor seals and cooks in about 20 minutes. The succulent fowl is ready when the skin is a golden chestnut color and the juices run clear. The leg should offer no resistance when pulled from its socket. If there is any doubt, test with a thermometer in a section of thigh meat that has not been pierced. It should read 175° F/330° C.

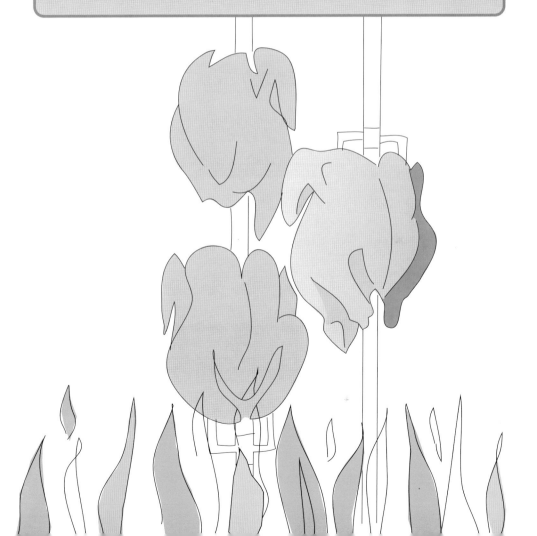

Marinating

This is basically soaking food in a liquid—usually containing oils and seasonings, and often vinegar, wine, citrus juice, or yogurt—to give extra taste to the food. Make sure that all the food is coated in the marinade, turning if necessary. You can use a self-sealing plastic bag. This makes it easy to turn the food. To reduce marinating time for meat when you are in a hurry, pound it with a mallet or rolling pin. Pierce the meat gently with a fork and add the marinade. Remember to use caution in the amount of sugar you add to marinated meat because a high sugar content is likely to burn more readily on the barbecue.

Marinating fish

When it comes to marinating fish, restrict the time to less than 2 hours to maintain its natural fresh taste. A marinade with an oil content will keep the fish moist and prevent sticking on a broiler surface. Marinating raw fish requires the freshest of ingredients due to bacteria concerns. Buy only from a reputable source. Many raw fish dishes call for citrus in the marinade. This acid in effect cooks the fish, though only in the sense that the flesh firms and whitens, and it enhances a fresh flavor. Prepare at the last minute and make sure to refrigerate raw fish dishes until just prior to serving.

Pouch cooking

Cook assorted vegetables in one pot by creating individual aluminum or baking parchment pouches and wrapping each kind individually. Begin with rectangular sheets. Fold the sheet over in half. Place the vegetables inside the fold. Add a little olive oil, herbs, and seasonings, if desired. Crease each of the open three sides and fold each twice over as though sealing an envelope. Add each to the boiling water based upon its relative cooking time. A complete meal can also be prepared in the same way. It is a very healthy method of cooking, given that all nutrients are retained and very little fat is involved. Use the same include y pouch, in and flavo

Dry-sal

This techn purposes fish such a salmon. Salt is rubbed into the flesh of the fish which then proceeds to draws out the juices. Fish takes about 1 week to dry-salt. Larger pieces of meat take longer to cure. The classic dry-cured ham takes 2 days for 1 lb/450 g of meat.

Salmon in a pouch

Serves 2

2 x 3–4 oz/75–115 g filets of salmon
½ cup/125 ml sherry or wine
1 tbsp extra-virgin olive oil
salt and pepper
1 clove garlic, minced
shallots

selection fresh herbs, such as chives, cilantro, dill, parsley, tarragon, or thyme, roughly cut
fennel
mushrooms
red bell peppers and/or tomatoes
cooked white beans

❶ Place a 3–4 oz/75 g–115 g filet of salmon on a piece of aluminum foil or baking parchment large enough to hold all the ingredients. Repeat with another filet of salmon.

❷ Add the sherry or wine, extra-virgin olive oil, salt, pepper, minced garlic, shallots, and a selection of roughly cut fresh herbs. Thinly slice fennel, mushrooms, red bell peppers, and/or tomatoes and place them in the envelope. Cooked white beans work nicely too. Make sure the envelopes are tightly sealed.

❸ Bake them in a preheated oven at 400° F/200° C/Gas 6 for 25 minutes. Remove the envelopes and after a few minutes, empty the contents into bowls as individual servings. Discard the foil and serve this delicious, still-steaming meal treat.

preparing & cooking food

fruit &
vegetables

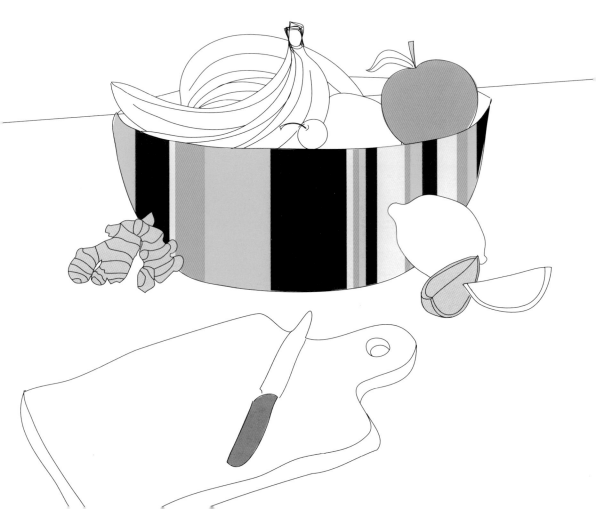

Fruit

Apple

Patchwork apples

Look for apples that have a bright, evenly colored background, and don't be put off by small brown patches. Hold the fruit and check for undesirable soft spots or holes.

Dry storage

They should be stored in a dry and cool place with their stem sides down. Avoid storing in the refrigerator. Other fruits and vegetables have a tendency to pick up their flavor when they are stored together.

Apple peel

Remove the peel on apples when they are waxed. Given its round shape, the skin can be removed in one long spiral with a peeler or paring knife. Quarter and core the apples for immediate consumption. If you plan on serving them later, store the pieces in water with a little fresh lemon juice.

Harvest apple sauce

Makes 4 cups/1¾ pints

8 apples
1 lemon, juice and zest
1 teaspoon powdered cinnamon

½ cup/100 g sugar
1 tsp pure vanilla extract

❶ Wash, quarter, and peel the apples. Core and remove the seeds. Remove the skin of the lemon with a zester or vegetable peeler, with as little of the white membrane as possible, and finely mince.

❷ Place the quartered apples in a saucepan with the lemon juice, zest, and cinnamon. Cover with a lid and cook for 30 minutes over a low heat. Stir and mash frequently as they begin to soften and render juice.

❸ Purée with a vegetable mill to an even consistency, or pulse in a

blender for a slightly chunkier style. Return the mixture to the pan and add the sugar. Depending on the tartness of the apples, you may wish to add more sugar to taste. Allow the sugar to dissolve and sauce to boil moderately.

❹ When the liquid has condensed, leaving a smooth sauce, remove from the heat and add the vanilla.

❺ Let stand to cool, then transfer to a sealed container. The apple sauce should keep for about 1 week.

Green bananas

Green bananas will ripen if stored at room temperature for a few days. When brown spots appear and they are supple but firm to the touch, they are ripe.

Keeping fresh

Store bananas at room temperature. Wrap them in a wet dishtowel for 10 minutes and place in a paper bag to promote ripening. Peeled bananas can be stored in the refrigerator sprinkled with a few drops of lemon juice and wrapped in aluminum foil.

Instant banana

Well-ripened bananas can be mashed with a little lemon, then frozen. This can be used for banana bread, cakes, fillings, as well as blended drinks.

Plantain

Recipes can call for ripened or green plantain. In any event, choose fruit that is firm and plump. Most likely there will be the appearance of blemishes, however these rarely penetrate to the fruit. Allow them to ripen at room temperature. When ripe, they may be refrigerated for up to 2 days. Blackening on the skin does not affect the flesh of the fruit.

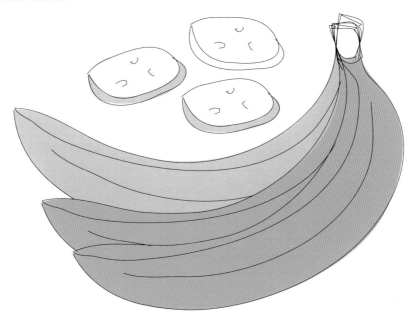

fruit & vegetables

Pear shopping

Choose pears with stems still attached. They should be firm, but slightly yielding at the top where the stem emerges.

Giving off gas

Pears (as with apples, plums, and tomatoes) give off ethanol gas, thus they should be stored separately. Pears (and plums) should be stored in a plastic bag or box in the fridge. From the time they are ripe, they may be stored for up to 10 days in the refrigerator. Fruit will keep better if they are not washed until removed from the refrigerator and before usage. If they are not ripe, they may be left at room temperature. Wrap them individually with newspaper and place in single layers to discourage bruising. Pears ripen faster in the company of apples.

Presenting a pear

Cut a pear in half lengthwise. Remove the core, seeds, and stem with a knife, leaving as much of the fruit intact as possible.

Stay in shape

If you are planning to poach whole pears, slice a thin piece away from the base. Take a melon baller and scoop out a circular core at the base. Leave the stem on for decorative purpose. In this manner, the pear will keep its shape when cooking.

Shake them down

When selecting grapes, look for plump and shiny fruit. Pick up the bunch and shake them gently. If some of them fall off the stem, it is questionable as to whether they are fresh.

Iced grapes

Grapes are best stored loosely in a linen towel or kitchen paper in the refrigerator vegetable crisper drawer. Loose frozen grapes or whole bunches that are wrapped and put in a sealed plastic bag can be removed from the freezer as required. This makes a refreshing, fruity treat in between meals.

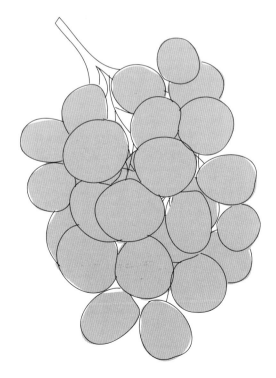

Keeping it cold

Whole ripe dessert melons can be stored at room temperature for up to 2 days. If they have been cut in half, they may be stored in the refrigerator for 3 additional days. Whole ripe watermelons can be stored at room temperature for up to 3 days. Halves and slices can be kept in the refrigerator for 1 week.

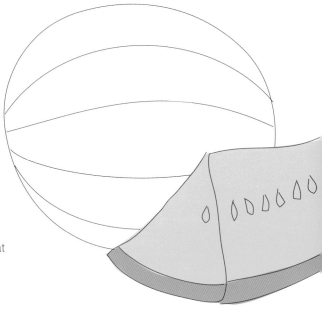

Serving it up

When serving halved fresh melon, slice a thin layer away from both the base and top of the melon, so that you may lay it flat on a plate. Cut the melon in half, parallel to the first slices. Scoop the seeds out from the cavities into a sieve laid over a bowl. The remaining juices may be retained for another use, or poured back into the cavities of the melon halves.

Sizing up melons

Hold the melon in your fingertips as though it were a ball. It should be quite heavy and firm. Press the area around the end where the stem existed. There should be a little give in the surface. If you are choosing between two of the same size, select the heaviest. A sweet scent should be noticeable from the stem side tip. Melons with cracks can often be the best. Thick, close netting on the rind of the cantaloupe indicates the best quality. When the stem scar is dry it is ripe. Honeydew is ripe when the rind has a creamy to yellow color and velvety texture. If the color is a white-green, it is not ripe. Watermelon should display some yellow color to one side. Avoid those with white or pale green coloration, and where the space between the netting is yellow to yellow-green.

fruit & vegetables

Muddled zest

For recipes calling for zest and sugar, add a small portion of the sugar to the prepared zest. Chop and blend together with a knife or food processor. The sugar begins to dissolve the zest and intensify the flavor, known as "muddling."

Newspaper wrap

Always store in a plastic bag in the refrigerator. If planning to store for more than 1 week, dry each fruit and individually wrap in newspaper before packing in the plastic bag or sealed container. If the lemon is cut, sprinkle a little salt or sugar on the exposed flesh to preserve longer.

Thin-skinned

The thinnest-skinned lemons are the most desirable. These are generally the juiciest. Choose as round a lemon as possible. The brighter the yellow color, the higher the vitamin C content will be in the fruit. Light or green-tinted lemons are more tart than deep yellow ones. Preferably the small brown knobs at the base and top should be intact. Avoid tiny limes. The more a lime resembles a lemon in size and color, the sweeter it will be. They should carry a heavy weight to indicate their juice content. Most skin markings do not affect quality. Avoid lemons and limes displaying withered, sunken, or soft areas.

Lemonade

Makes 4 glasses

6 large lemons, juice only
4 cups/1 liter water
2 cups/450 g sugar

fresh mint sprigs and lemon slice wheels, to garnish

1 Clean the whole lemons thoroughly with a coarse vegetable brush to release the oils. Cut each lemon in half and squeeze the juice into a pot.

2 Add the water and bring to the boil. Pour in the sugar and stir until it is dissolved. Add the lemons to the mixture.

3 Mash down with a wooden spoon. Set aside to cool. Cover and place in the refrigerator overnight.

4 Strain the liquid from the solid matter into a pitcher before serving. Pour the lemonade into each glass with a few cubes of ice, and garnish with a lemon slice wheel and sprig of fresh mint.

Squeezing juice

Citrus fruit will yield the most juice if allowed to stand at room temperature first. Roll the fruit on a hard surface with the palm of your hand. Pierce the meat of the fruit with a fork before squeezing the juice. One lemon yields approximately ¼ cup/60 ml juice. One orange yields about ⅓ cup/75 ml juice.

Slicing and peeling

If you are slicing wedges, slice away the pith or white membrane from the inner edge to avoid squirting and allow for ease in squeezing. If you are peeling oranges and want to remove the bitter white membrane between the flesh and the skin, soak the whole fruit in warm water first for 15 minutes. Dry and remove the skin. To cut the orange into slices, use a serrated bread knife.

Ice cream shells

Empty shells from citrus fruit halves or zest can be reserved and frozen in a plastic bag and saved for future use. The halves can be used as hollows for ice cream desserts, and the zest can be used in cooking preparations in combination with herbs for savory items and spices for sweet sauces.

In the refrigerator

Always store citrus fruits in a plastic bag in the refrigerator. If planning to store them for more than 1 week, dry each fruit and individually wrap in newspaper before packing in the plastic bag or sealed container.

Zest ideas

Grate the zest from unpeeled fruit for flavoring sauces and desserts. To make strips of zest, peel the skin away in long strips. Dice the zest for cooking preparations, or curl long strands to garnish drinks.

How orange?

The color of the orange is not the most important feature. It should be firm with no blemishes. When the fruit has a protruding, rounded form at the bottom, almost resembling a smaller formation, the orange will most likely be sweet and juicy. Oranges with a slight green tinge may be just as ripe as fully colored ones. The thinnest-skinned oranges are the most desirable. These are generally the juiciest.

Orange terrine

Serves 6

5 large oranges
2½ cups/600 ml fresh orange juice
¼ cup/50 g granulated sugar
6 sheets leaf gelatine

❶ Remove the peel of each orange and cut into segments. Heat the orange juice and sugar in a saucepan to nearly boiling, until the sugar has dissolved. Remove from heat and stir in gelatine until dissolved. Let cool.

❷ Lightly oil a 5-cup/1.2-liter capacity terrine mold and layer orange segments across the bottom until it is three-quarters full. Pour in orange juice and allow to set for 6 hours. Turn out.

The meaning of hulls

Look for whether the hull remains on the top of the berries. In strawberries this is fine, but with other berries it probably means they have been picked when they were under ripe. Attached leaves and hulls should be green and fresh and the color and aroma should be intense. The form should be plump, and there should be no sign of shriveling or mold.

The delicate touch

Delicate berries that need to be washed may be rinsed with gently running cool water through a colander. Dry flat on paper towels. Berries can last a few additional days if stored unwashed in a colander with the possibility for air to circulate. Soft berries may also be stored on a baking sheet lined with paper towels. Remove any that are moldy or damaged and loosely cover with another layer of paper toweling, then refrigerate.

Snap frozen

Berries will last up to a year in the freezer. If they are sprinkled with sugar, they will maintain a more intense aroma. Berries are likely to change in consistency to varying degrees. By placing them on a baking sheet first, they can also be frozen separately, as opposed to in a lump. Open-freeze them until they are completely firm, then they can be stored in a container or plastic bag together. If whole frozen berries are being used as a garnish for a cake, for example, allow them to thaw for 30 minutes in place before consuming. As an alternative, consider making a berry purée. This is great for toppings for ice cream, making smoothies, or filling for pies and cakes.

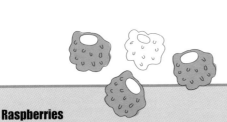

Raspberries

Select berries that are plump, moist, and deep in color. Check for intensity of fragrance and avoid raspberries that appear to be clustered together. To rid raspberries of the small insects that tend to live within their cavities, place them in a covered container in the refrigerator. Once the container has had the opportunity to cool, the insects should migrate to the bottom of the closed lid.

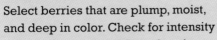

fruit & vegetables

Sweeteners

Squeeze a little lemon juice over berries, particularly blueberries and strawberries. This will intensify the flavor. Sugar will also intensify the flavor, but will begin to diminish the firmness of the fruit. Use superfine sugar to sprinkle over the berries and let them stand at room temperature for 30 minutes. A concentrated flavor and light syrup will develop. Berries that have become a bit soft can be mashed or puréed in a food processor. Add the purée to yogurt or spoon over vanilla ice cream for dessert.

Strawberries

Remove the hull at the top of a strawberry with flat-end tweezers. Work at the base of the leafy stem and pull outwards, discouraging the running of juice or unnecessarily wasting any flesh of the fruit. When they lack full flavor, cut them horizontally to expose more surface space. It will promote the flow of juices.

Raspberry purée

For a simple raspberry purée that complements pastries or ice cream, use cooked fresh or thawed frozen berries. Purée in the food processor or a blender to a smooth consistency. Press through a fine sieve or strainer to collect the tiny seeds and create a velvety texture. You may add confectioner's sugar to sweeten, and a liquor, such as framboise, to flavor and/or thin the purée to your liking.

Checking for ripeness

Pick peaches, plums, and nectarines that feel heavy for their size, as the weight is a sign of juiciness. The skin should be smooth, unblemished, and yield to your touch, whilst giving off a sweet aroma. To speed up the ripening process, store at room temperature in a brown paper bag.

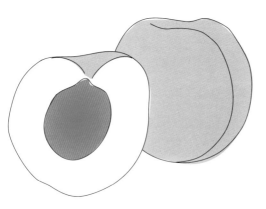

Stone fruit pits

To remove the pit, cut along the natural indentation of the fruit in a full circle from the stem side, as close to the stone as possible. Hold the fruit in both hands and twist the two halves gently apart. Pluck out the pit with the end of the knife. To remove the skins before cutting the fruit, drop into boiling water for 45 seconds. Remove the fruit and plunge into an ice-cold water bath. When they have cooled, pat them dry with a cloth and remove the skins with the tip of a paring knife. If you are not using the fruit immediately, return it to a cold water bath with a little lemon juice.

Apricot

Splitting the apricot

Find the indentation on the surface and use it as a guide for cutting the apricot in half. Give the halves a sharp twist with both hands to separate them. If the flesh sticks to the pit, use a paring knife to loosen it. After plucking out the pit, you can peel the fruit.

Apricots in liqueur

Serves 4

fruit brandy liqueur
1 lemon, juice only

8 whole fresh apricots, washed

❶ Pour fruit brandy or liqueur and a little lemon juice over the apricots to half cover them.

❷ Cover in a heat-resistant dish and microwave on high for 5 minutes. Turn over halfway through the cooking time.

❸ When they are still warm, slip off the skins and serve in the juice. If you don't have a microwave, poach the same mixture in a pan until the fruit is tender. Leftovers can be served on cold vanilla ice cream after removing the pits.

Spooning it out

Slice off the stem end top of the kiwi. Take a spoon and spoon out the flesh away from, and as close to, the skin as possible. Try to keep it in a nicely rounded whole form. Cut into round slices or wedges.

Peeling the skin

If it becomes difficult to peel the skin away, place the fruit in boiling water for a minute. Pat dry and remove the skin.

Pineapple rings

Slice away the outer skin of a ripe pineapple. Remove any remaining brown eyespots. Slice the meat of the fruit into rings. Use an appropriate-sized cookie cutter ring to remove the central core. You can shape the outer sides to a uniform size with a larger cookie cutter ring. Alternatively, it is possible to buy a special tool that peels, cores, and slices pineapple in no time at all, leaving the shell intact for use as a dessert or serving bowl.

Just ripe

The coloring should be yellow brown, preferably with no trace of green on the skin. If you can pull out a leaf from the top of the fruit with ease, this is an indication that it is ripe. There should also be some give to the flesh of the fruit when pressed with the fingertips. A fruity aroma should be present at the base of the pineapple. When you take the pineapple home, ripen at room temperature, then store in the refrigerator.

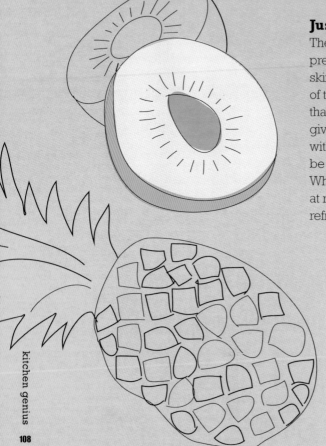

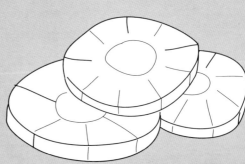

Mango

Mango ripeness

It is difficult to gauge the ripeness of a mango by its color as the color differs with each variety. Mangoes that are under ripe often have an unpleasant chemical taste when eaten in their raw state. Do not buy the fruit if it does not give off a floral, fragrant aroma, as it will most likely have no flavor. Hold it in the palm of your hand and gently squeeze. The mango is most likely to be ripe if you can feel a slight give in the flesh. Once purchased, mangoes should be ripened at room temperature and then stored at 35° F/2° C.

How to eat?

Hold the mango horizontally on a flat surface. Cut it lengthwise across, just missing the seed. Repeat with the opposite side, leaving a thin layer of flesh around the seed. Cut the remaining layer of fruit away from the seed. Slice crisscross squares into the flesh of these pieces, without cutting through the skin. Create a curvature to the skin and slice away the cubes as close to the skin as possible. Don't waste any flesh from the delicious mango. Suck the seed with the remaining flesh as a refreshing snack.

Chili mango salsa

Serves 4

1 large mango
1 small red onion, very finely chopped
1 red chili, deseeded and finely chopped

1 lime, juice only
2 tbsp fresh chopped mint
2 tbsp fresh chopped cilantro

❶ Peel and finely dice the mango flesh and put into a non-reactive bowl. Add the onion, chili, and lime juice. Season lightly and toss together to mix. Set aside until needed.

❷ Add the mint and cilantro to the salsa and mix well.

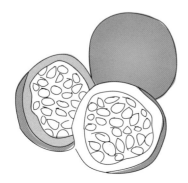

Pomegranate

Pomegranate segments

Divide the fruit into segments by slicing through the skin to the center. Pull back the wedges and scoop out the seeds with a spoon, discarding the skin and white membrane pith.

Dried fruits

Plumping up

Always look for dried fruits that have a good deep color and are soft and springy to the touch. Dried fruits, such as figs, raisins, and prunes, may be stored in a closed container with a dried bay leaf. Pack loosely and keep in a cool dry place to help maintain a supple and soft texture. If raisins become hard in storage, place them in a bowl of boiling water and let stand for 15 minutes. Drain and dry them before use.

Dates

Rinsing dates for a few moments in hot running water can rejuvenate dried dates that have begun to crystallize or have a dull-colored surface. Pat them dry with a towel and serve immediately.

Snipping

Snip dried fruits into pieces using scissors. If the blades become sticky, dip them in a glass of hot water and continue to snip. Soaking dried fruits in aromatic herb teas can plump them up for use in quick breads or cakes. Dried fruits remain moist and are also easier to cut when stored in the freezer. When blending dried fruits, add a little sugar to prevent the fruits sticking to the blades of the food processor.

Overnight breakfast

Place dried fruits in a bowl with a little boiled fruit juice. Cover with a plate and set in the refrigerator overnight. This mixture can be added to muesli or served as breakfast compote in the morning.

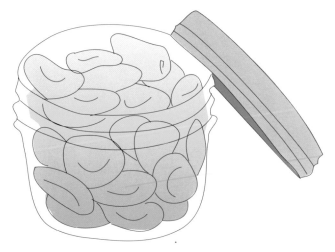

Peeling the tomato

To peel whole tomatoes, blanch in boiling water for 1 minute. Submerge in a bath of cold water and remove the skins with ease. If your recipe calls for deseeding tomatoes, scoop the seeds out with a teaspoon. Squeezing tomatoes makes the flesh mushy.

Firm and smooth

Select tomatoes that are firm not soft. The surface should be smooth and have no splits. Vine-ripened tomatoes exude a fresh, vegetal fragrance.

Tomato frenzy

If you have a glut of tomatoes, peel them using the method opposite. Freeze whole and seal them in covered containers. To use, remove from the freezer and chop them while they are still frozen. Use them in sauces and soups.

Mash or chop

Choose either to mash or chop tomatoes before freezing when harvesting or buying in large quantities.

Not too hot

Simmer whole tomatoes slowly to avoid bursting. Tomatoes cooked at high temperatures will burst if whole and the acidity content will be more intense.

Fruit and vegetable juices

Juices can be stored in the freezer and defrosted as needed. To promote thawing, whizz the contents of a carton or container in the food processor.

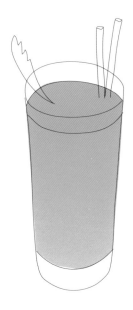

Tomato sauce for pasta

Makes 2 cups/475ml

2 cloves garlic, minced
3 medium onions, chopped
1 large carrot, finely chopped
2 stalks celery, finely chopped,
or ½ cup/60 g finely chopped
celery root
5 tbsp extra-virgin olive oil
½ cup/125 ml dry red wine
(preferably the wine being served
with the meal)

2 lb/900 g fresh or canned
peeled, seeded, and chopped
tomatoes
1 tsp dried Greek oregano
(preferably from the stem)
sea salt and freshly ground black
pepper
1 tsp sugar (optional)
3 tbsp each of fresh basil and
Italian (flat-leaf) parsley, coarsely
chopped

❶ Begin by sautéing the garlic, onion, carrot, and celery in the olive oil until tender and the onion is translucent.

❷ Add the wine and reduce to half the amount of liquid.

❸ Add the tomatoes, oregano, salt, pepper, and sugar, if using.

❹ Simmer and stir regularly over low heat for about 30 minutes, or until the sauce thickens to your desired consistency.

❺ Add the fresh basil and parsley to the sauce just before serving.

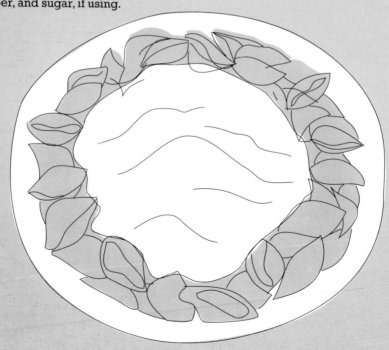

Not too cool

Do not store in the refrigerator until fully ripe, and throw out when they become mushy and watery in texture at cold temperatures. The ripening process is also arrested. If ripe, tomatoes can also be stored in an open paper bag or egg carton where it's cool and dark. If they are not ripe, store them in a paper bag with an apple or a ripened tomato for about 3 days. To test for ripeness, hold the tomato gently in the palm of your hand and apply pressure softly. The tomato will give slightly if it is ready to be eaten.

Tomato garnish
Create a tomato floret garnish by setting the tomato down on a cutting board and slicing it into sixths from the center. Cut down only to ¼ inch/ 5 mm from the bottom, and spread the "petals" out gently.

Avocado

Ripe?
Whether the surface is flat or textured, choose an avocado that is ripe. Hold it in the palm of your hand and close gently to feel if there is give. Harsh squeezing can cause bruising. Avocados being sliced and used in salads should be a bit firm. When ripening avocados at home, one can determine readiness by inserting a toothpick at the base. If the pick moves through the flesh with ease, it is ripe. A dark green to black color also indicates that the avocado is likely to be ripe.

Stay green
Ripe avocados should be stored in the refrigerator. If unripe, they may be placed with an apple in a plastic bag until ready. Gases from the apple will accelerate the ripening process. If you are using only half an avocado, you can retain the stone in the unused part and seal in a plastic bag. This will inhibit discoloration. By the same token, when making guacamole, retain the stones and if you find yourself with any leftover, embed the stones on the surface and plastic wrap the top of the bowl snugly. This should stop the browning.

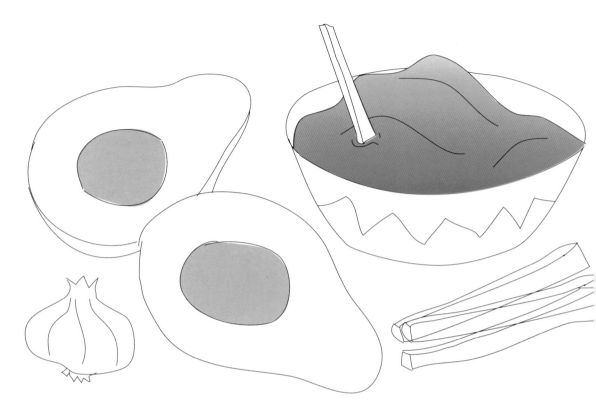

Scooping out the flesh

Cut the avocado in half lengthwise along the seed. Remove the seed without pulling out the inner flesh by tapping the blade of a knife into the seed and twisting gently to remove. Take a spoon and scoop out the flesh from the wide end first, being careful to work along the skin as closely as possible. Cut away any discolored parts. Protect from discoloration and enhance the flavor by squeezing fresh lime juice over the surface.

Chunky guacamole

2 ripe avocados, Hass, if possible
2 plum tomatoes, seeded and diced
1 clove garlic, crushed
3 green onions, finely chopped

Serves 4

1 lemon, juice only
1 cup cilantro, coarsely chopped
3 tbsp sour cream, plus extra to serve

① Cut the avocados in half lengthwise and remove the stone. Peel and roughly chop the flesh, then mash coarsely in a mixing bowl.

② Add the tomatoes, garlic, green onions, lemon juice, cilantro, and sour cream. Season to taste.

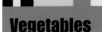

Vegetables

Lettuce

Lettuce wash

To remove the core of an iceberg lettuce, bang the core side down on the counter. Move it in a circular motion. You should be able to extract the core by twisting it out in a repeated circular motion. To wash the entire head of lettuce, run cold water into the opened cavity. Submerge the cored end down into a bath of cold water. Let it rest for about 20 minutes. Rejuvenate a tired lettuce by trimming the stem end and leaving it in icy water for 5 minutes before preparation. Tear the leaves of delicate greens into bite-size pieces, rather than cutting them with a knife.

Heavy and firm

Hold the lettuce in your hand to feel for heaviness. Press in both hands with your fingertips to select one with firmness and density. Avoid any with discoloration.

Wash and dry

Once the lettuce or other salad greens have been washed, they can be wrapped in kitchen paper towels, placed in a plastic bag, and set in the vegetable crisper drawer.

Types of salad greens

• Tightly packed iceberg and butterhead, or bibb and Boston, are two of the most commonly used lettuces. The first is noted primarily for its crunchy texture, whereas the latter for its flavor and delicacy.

• Belgian endive, frisée, and radicchio have a peppery flavor and a sturdier structure.

• Arugula is also a long-leafed green with a distinctive bitter punch. Use it with milder flavored greens or with a sweet and acidic mixed dressing.

• Romaine is a long-leaf lettuce, which also has a crispy texture and is generally mild in taste.

• Red oakleaf lettuce is looser in composition and adds color to a salad composition.

• Mâche is probably the most delicate of greens, and one of the first to emerge in the spring. Due to its mild flavor it can balance the taste of stronger greens. It is commonly used in braising, in addition to providing taste and texture to more delicately flavored salads.

fruit & vegetables

Salad extras

To make a salad extra special:

• Sprinkle slivered almonds, salted peanuts, or toasted sunflower seeds over your salad for extra crunch.

• Use a vegetable peeler to make long, wide curls from a Parmesan wedge to top your salad.

• Add lots of fresh herbs for flavor. Consider snipped chives, whole leaves of basil, chervil, oregano, or thyme, and rough-cut cilantro and mint. Only the simplest of oil and vinegar or lemon-based dressings is necessary.

Endive

Kept in the dark

Never expose to light to prevent added bitterness. Store in an opaque plastic bag in the refrigerator.

No soaking

Brush the endive clean for salads, but do not soak in water. For cooked endive, boil it unwashed in water. To remove some of the bitterness, add a little salt or milk to the boiling water.

Bitter taste

Endive is in the chicory family and may be used raw in a salad mix to introduce a slight bitter flavor, or braised as a side vegetable. When shopping for this green, look for crisp, tightly packed heads with a fresh smell. Avoid those with browning discoloration, and select ones with an even pale-yellow green hue.

Celery

Stringy

Remove the tough, stringy surface from the outer stalks of celery by first separating each one individually from the heart. Using a vegetable peeler, run it down the outer length of each stalk. Peel the outer layer of the heart and add this to the inner stalks and leaves to flavor soups and stock.

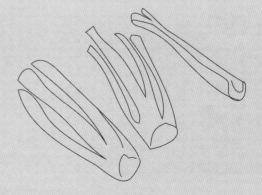

Slender elegance

Choose long, straight, and slender cucumbers for the best quality. Dark to medium green is the desired color, while yellowed are over ripe.

Cool but not icy

Wrap cucumbers entirely in plastic wrap when storing in the refrigerator vegetable crisper drawer. Avoid contact with tomatoes and apples. Cucumbers cannot be frozen.

Seeding and slicing

The skin of the cucumber is more difficult to digest than the inside, so peel it away if you desire. Cut the whole cucumber lengthwise. Take a teaspoon or melon ball scooper and run it down the middle to remove the seeds, then slice for a salad. To remove excess water and bitterness, place the slices in a shallow dish and sprinkle with coarse salt. The salt will extract the excess water in 15 minutes. The texture should firm up in addition. Drain and use in salad.

Salad dressing

• Avoid astringency in sweet vinegar dressings by substituting a portion with fresh orange juice or adding a little honey.

• Warm salads can be tossed with a little balsamic vinegar for extra flavor.

• Use a few drops of sesame oil as a condiment to dress Asian-style salads.

• Add drained, finely chopped anchovies to potato salad for additional flavor.

• Replace oil with plain yogurt to create a lower-fat dressing.

• Mash ripe Roquefort or blue cheese with equal parts mayonnaise and sour cream for a creamy dressing.

• The basis of a vinaigrette is 3 parts oil to 1 part vinegar, or 5 part oil to 1 part lemon juice. Use a clean glass jar with a screw top lid to shake it up. If it contains only oil, vinegar, and mustard, it will last several weeks refrigerated.

• A dressing will last 1 week if you have added dried herbs. Vinaigrettes that contain fresh herbs, garlic, or minced vegetables will survive only a few days in the refrigerator.

Beets

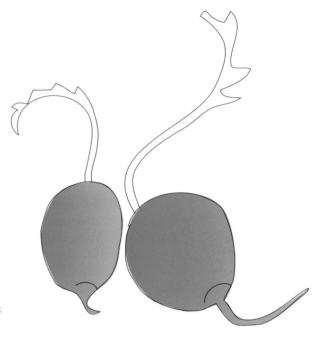

Boiling whole

Remove dirt and scrub the root
vegetable under cold running water.
To avoid an undesirable woody taste,
boil beets with their skin, roots, and
tops on. This will prevent the leakage
of juice and color as well.

Raw

Beets can be eaten raw. Add peeled and
grated beets to salads, sandwiches or as
an accompaniment to other vegetables.

Herbs

Delicate herbs

Five herbs that have delicate leaves and
are best when they have just been picked
include basil, chervil, mint, parsley, and
tarragon. Rough chop these leaves for a
confetti garnish, or add to a mixed salad.
They are at their optimum flavor raw.

Fresh, fresh herbs

Select fresh herbs before the flowering
process begins, when the most flavoring
is concentrated in the leaves. Herbs
should have a fresh aromatic scent and no
sign of mustiness. Shake the stems, which
in no way should show any signs of
wilting, and make sure that the leaves stay
intact. Choose outdoor-grown varieties
rather than greenhouse-house grown
when available.

Treating them carefully

Delicate fresh herbs, such as basil, cilantro, dill, leaf parsley, and tarragon, may be
stored for up to a week in the refrigerator. Separate each stem and remove all
discolored leaves. Slice off the tips on the bias and set the stems down in a glass of
water with a dissolved ½ teaspoon sugar. Loosely wrap in plastic wrap and refrigerate.
Do not rinse herbs until just before using. If you have purchased the herb with root
intact, cilantro for example, do not remove it as described above. Roots and stems of
herbs can be reserved, and thoroughly washed for stocks. Cilantro and flat-leaf parsley
roots add nutritional value and intensity to the flavor.

Robust herbs

Robust herbs, such as bay leaf, marjoram, oregano, rosemary, sage, and thyme, are sturdier and can withstand a colder growing season. Their flavors mellow when dried. Also, they can withstand higher cooking temperature and add depth in flavor and appealing aroma to prepared dishes.

Parsley alternatives

Consider garnishing plates with alternatives to parsley. Select fresh sprigs of chervil, chives, cilantro, flowering basil, tarragon, or thyme.

Bouquet garni

Use a mortar and pestle to bruise and release oils from the herbs and spices with which you plan to flavor your soup or stew. Wrap the mixture in cheesecloth and tie it with string to avoid loose floating bits. If you don't have cheesecloth, use a securely fastened tea ball strainer.

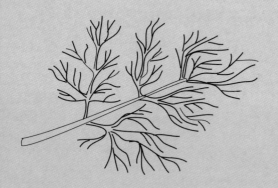

Dill

Tired dill wakes up if you submerge the ends in boiling water for a few moments.

Basil

When basil is in season, prepare an abundance of pesto that will last a year. Wrap and seal in various portion sizes in the freezer.

Parsley

When selecting a bunch of parsley, it should be freshly picked, as evident by its deep green color and pungent aroma. Leaves and stems should appear well formed and lively. Flat leaf or Italian parsley is more tasty in its raw form, and serves as a perfect accent of color and flavor for finished dishes when it is coarsely or finely chopped. Choose curly parsley for deep-frying, such as when making tempura. Curly parsley and its roots are widely used in preparations of stocks, soups, and stews. When freshly cut, set stems down in water with plastic wrap around the top of the glass and change the water daily. The big stems from parsley can be finely chopped and place in a sealed container or freezer bag. Add to soups, stews, or as a garnish, without needing to defrost first.

Herby seeds

Some herbs, such as cilantro, dill, and fennel, are favored for their leaves, eaten raw, and at the same time their seeds, which are dried and used as spices. When roasted the seeds give off their aroma. They are used in cooked dishes. In the case of cilantro, its seed, known as coriander, has a totally different taste.

Edible flowers
Nasturtiums are one example of edible flowers that impart a mild taste and create a dramatic contrast of color in fresh garden salads and open-faced sandwiches.

Pesto

Makes 2 cups/475 ml

1½ cups/75 g firmly packed fresh basil leaves
4 cloves garlic, sliced
⅓ cup/50 g pine nuts
¼ cup/30 g walnuts

½ cup/50 g grated Parmesan cheese
¼ cup/25 g grated sharp pecorino
sea salt and freshly ground black pepper
¾ cup/185 ml extra-virgin olive oil

❶ Prepare the pesto with a mortar and pestle or, for speed and convenience, with a food processor. In either case, mix all the ingredients together with the paste except for the oil.

❷ Pour the oil in gradually as you integrate the other ingredients so that the sauce emulsifies.

❸ Pour into a sterilized glass jar; add a little extra oil to float on the top as a sealer, and cover with a lid. It should last for up to 2 weeks in the refrigerator.

Artichokes

Leaves and stems

Globe artichokes should have compacted green heads with an absence of dry streaks and dark patches. The young variety is smaller with softer leaves and stem. A wide diameter at the base is more important than the actual size. Avoid choosing those with spread leaves, as this indicates age and tougher texture.

Vegetable flowers

Treat them like cut flowers and place them in water, base down. Change the water daily.

Jerusalem artichokes

Boil the roots whole without peeling. You should be able to rub the skins off easily after cooking, thus saving time and labor.

Squeeze of lemon

To fortify the flavor of cooked artichokes, add the juice of a half squeezed lemon, a tablespoon olive oil, and a teaspoon sugar to boiling water. Use a non-reactive pan like a porcelain-clad pan, cast-iron, or stainless steel. Artichokes have a tendency to darken if cooked in aluminum.

Globe artichokes

Remove the stem from the bottom of the artichoke by breaking it off and pulling out excess fibers. Slice off about ½ inch/ 1 cm from the base so that it sits flat. Cut off about ½ inch/1 cm from the top of the artichoke, and snip off the remaining pointed leaf tips with scissors. Set the prepared artichokes in a large pan with shallow salted boiling water. Weight them down with a heat-resistant plate so that they do not move. Simmer slowly for 45 minutes, or until you can pull out one of the center leaves with ease.

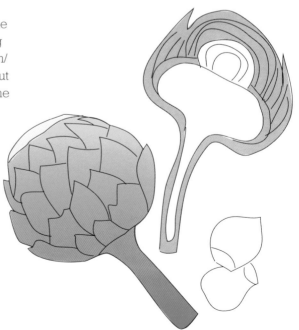

Asparagus

Water and steam

Create a ring with aluminum foil on the inside of a cooking pot, leaving the center free to stand the asparagus upright, stems down in the boiling water. The stems will cook in the water and the steam will cook the tops.

Breaking point

To determine what part of the asparagus to discard or to use for stock, take the asparagus spear in both hands and bend it. It will break at a point that determines the woody part you should then set aside for stock or discard. Use a vegetable peeler to remove the outer layer of the stem on each spear.

Green and white

Stalks should be plump, firm, and uniform in shape. Tips should be close and compact. Select asparagus with very little white in the stalks. The thicker stalks are generally more tender. Use asparagus quickly from the time of purchase because it toughens rapidly. White asparagus is seasonally available and generally more expensive. It is harvested colorless, with a white or pale yellow hue, because it is picked before it sprouts above the ground. Its taste is more piquant than green asparagus.

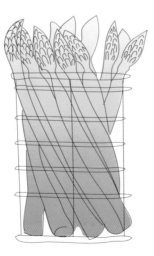

Baby vegetables

Many types of vegetables are available in dwarf form or as regular varieties that are picked at an early stage of development. Sometimes they are more tender and sweet, as is the case with zucchini and patty pan squash. Others may lack the intensity of flavor of the mature vegetable, as may be the case with finger-length corn. Scrub baby vegetables thoroughly in cold running water, but don't peel them. Their skins have a high nutritional value and fiber. Retain ¼ inch/5 mm of the baby carrot and turnip tops to add a variation in color and texture.

Extra storage

To store for an extra 3 days, remove the band from the bunch and cut approximately ½ inch/1 cm off the bottom of each stalk. Give the stalks a warm water bath for about 30 minutes. Fill a glass-measuring cup with 3 inches/8 cm of cold water and place the stalks in. Cover the top loosely with plastic wrap and set in the refrigerator. You can sustain the life longer if you change the water in the glass every other day, and rinse off the submerged ends in cold water. You can also revive tired asparagus by submerging the stems in icy cold water.

Canned asparagus
If the asparagus is in a can, open it from the bottom so as not to damage the tops.

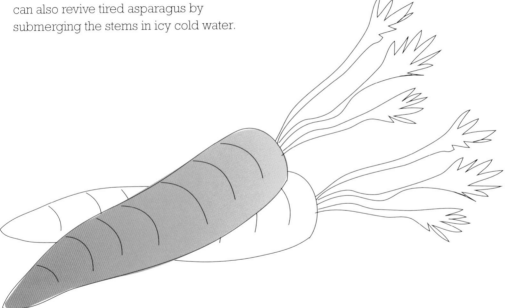

Carrots

Crisper carrots

Remove all green tops from carrots as these draw moisture and vitamins from the root, causing the carrot to toughen and wilt. Carrots need cold temperatures and high humidity, so store them wrapped in plastic in the vegetable crisper.

Bright orange

If the carrots are intensely orange, they are of good quality. It is better to buy many smaller carrots as opposed to large. The large varieties can be tougher. Carrots are available throughout the year, but are at their sweetest and most tender when they are smaller in early summer.

Broccoli

Tight clusters

Select broccoli that are a deep green with no signs of flowering or beginning to turn yellow. Flower clusters should be tight and close together.

Cooking

Separate the stalks from the florets after washing. Slice away the woody base tip and remove the surface of the stalk with a vegetable peeler. Slice the stalks into ¼ inch/5 mm rings and cook until "al dente" with the florets.

Stand up

Remove the rubber band and cut ½ inch/1 cm off the end of a broccoli stalk. Stand the broccoli up in a glass of cold water and cover the floret top loosely with plastic. The broccoli should last about 1 week in the refrigerator.

Spinach

Getting the grit

To wash the grit and sand from spinach, make a cold water bath and add 1 tablespoon of coarse salt. Let it soak for 30 minutes. The dirt should sink to the bottom. Lift the greens and rinse through a colander.

Cooking

Boiled spinach should be drained in a colander, shaken, and pressed with the flat end of a spoon to drive any remaining liquid out. As an alternative, cleaned spinach can be rapidly sautéed in a little butter or olive oil. This takes only a few moments when the pan is hot. Serve when tender.

Brussels sprouts

Super sprouts

Look for sprouts that are deep green with no yellowing or indication of brown spots. Try to select those that are firm, compact, and uniform in shape and size for even cooking.

Flavor aging

The flavor will intensify with age, so it is recommended to store Brussels sprouts for no more than 4 days in a sealed bag or container in the refrigerator. If they are blanched and frozen, they will keep for up to 1 year.

Cut a cross

Cut a cross into the bottom of each stem to promote even cooking.

Brussels sprouts in pecan sauce

Serves 4–6

1 lb/450 g Brussels sprouts, trimmed
3 tbsp butter, unsalted
¼ cup/25 g pecans, chopped
salt and freshly ground black pepper, to taste

1 Cook sprouts in boiling salted water until tender for about 10 minutes. Drain and keep warm.

2 Heat butter in small saucepan and brown the pecans, being careful not to burn them. Pour pecans over sprouts and serve.

Cauliflower

Insect-free

Inspect the cauliflower by pulling back the outer leaves. Make sure that there are no signs of decay or small insects between and on the outer edges of the florets. There should be an overall creamy white color and firm texture. Refrigerate in loose plastic wrap for up to 4 days.

Pure white

Retain cauliflower's white color when cooking by not adding salt to the water. For the ultimate white color, cook it in milk, or add a little white vinegar to the water when boiling.

fruit & vegetables

Stock-boiled

Finely shredded cabbage can be simmered in a shallow amount of stock rather than water for additional flavor. There should be enough to just cover the surface. Stir until tender.

Try steaming

An alternative method to preparing cabbage involves slicing the head into wedges. Place in a steamer and cook until tender. This method will preserve more of the nutrients.

Saving time

You can eliminate blanching by putting a whole head of cabbage in the freezer overnight. Thaw at room temperature for 30 minutes before you are ready to use. This will wilt the leaves to the desired pliable texture for stuffing.

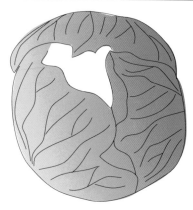

Hole-free cabbages

Avoid buying cabbages that have holes in the outer leaves or discolored brown patches. Hold the cabbage in your hand and gently press towards the center with the other. The heart should be firm.

Stuffing

If you plan to use cabbage leaves for stuffing, blanch them in boiling water first until pliable. Drain, dry, and flatten the rib down the center of the leaf with the flat end of a knife so that it can be rolled with ease. Stuff the cabbage leaves with a savory stuffing and roll them into neat parcels, then bake according to recipe.

Bulk buying

Cabbage, like other hearty greens such as collard, kale, and spinach, can be bought in bulk for freezing. Clean them thoroughly, cut if desired, and steam until tender. Freeze them in their own liquid in sealed containers or bags. Use them in soups or as side dishes.

Odor-free

Onions can be chopped and frozen. It is particularly important to store in a sealed container to ensure no lingering odors.

Dark and dry

Store onions in a cool, dry, and dark location. Peeled onions should be wrapped in aluminum foil and set in the refrigerator. The fleshy surface of a cut onion should be brushed with oil before being covered and put away. If your preparation requires only a portion of the onion, retain the root end, wrap in plastic wrap, and store in the refrigerator for up to 3 days.

Mild and sweet

Soak cut raw onion in cold water for 1 hour before adding to salads. Some varieties of onions may have a strong flavor, but this method diminishes the intensity. Slowly sauté chopped onions in butter to a nice golden brown color. This caramelized sweetness will add a terrific flavor to sauces. Boil onions faster by scoring an x-shape into the root-based end.

Bronzed onions

Select firm, bronze-colored onions that are round in shape and shiny on the surface. Avoid picking those with dried skins or signs of sprouting at the top.

French onion soup

Serves 4

2 tbsp olive oil
1 tbsp butter
2 bay leaves
1 lb/450 g onions, sliced
5 cups/1.25 liters homemade stock

salt and freshly ground black pepper
8 thick slices of French bread
1 cup/120 g grated Gruyère cheese
2 tbsp dry sherry

❶ Heat the oil and butter in a large saucepan. Add the bay leaves and onions. Stir well to coat the onions in the oil and butter, then cook, stirring occasionally, for 20–30 minutes, until the onions are browned.

❷ Add the stock and a little seasoning. Bring to the boil, reduce the heat, and cover the pan. Simmer gently for 30 minutes.

❸ Just before the soup is ready, preheat the broiler. Toast the bread on one side. Top the untoasted sides with the cheese and broil until melted, bubbling, and golden. Stir the sherry into the soup, taste it for seasoning, and ladle into warmed bowls. Add two slices of toasted cheese on bread to each portion and serve at once.

fruit & vegetables

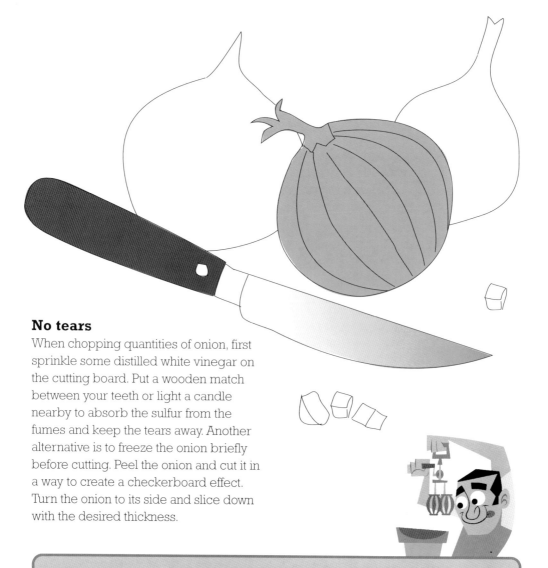

No tears

When chopping quantities of onion, first sprinkle some distilled white vinegar on the cutting board. Put a wooden match between your teeth or light a candle nearby to absorb the sulfur from the fumes and keep the tears away. Another alternative is to freeze the onion briefly before cutting. Peel the onion and cut it in a way to create a checkerboard effect. Turn the onion to its side and slice down with the desired thickness.

Green and red onions

An alternative to the common onion is the sweet onion. Two varieties, the Bermuda and the Vidalia, are favored for being eaten raw, whether it is in salads or sandwiches. They are frequently as strong in flavor as more common yellow types. Italian, or red, onions are noted for their sweet flavor, are also eaten raw or used instead of milder white and yellow varieties. Tiny pearl onions are cherry-tomato size and favored for pickling or as garnishes for soups and stews. Similar in flavor is the long and slender green onion, or scallion. It has a strong, grassy taste, which complements softer and sweeter greens and vegetables, both raw and ever so slightly cooked. Its bright green-colored stalk and immature bulb provide the necessary crunch and color to many dishes.

Tall and straight

Look for firm-textured stalks and bulbs with vivid green tops. There should be no evidence of dryness or slimy residue on the leaves.

Clean up

Cut the root end away from the bottom. Cut the top away to the point where the inside is a bright yellow green. Do not use the dark green outer layer. Slice the leek into rings of the desired width and soak in cold water with a little salt. This will remove the dirt efficiently. Drain well.

Instant leeks

Wrap leeks in paper and store in the refrigerator. For quick use in soups and stews, they may be cleaned, cut in rings, and stored in the freezer in an airtight plastic container.

Potato

Skin on

Select potatoes that are uniform in size as they will cook in the same time when boiled or baked whole. If the skin is thin on red and white potatoes, peeling is unnecessary. These may be boiled with the skins intact and thus retain beneficial nutrients.

Toxic green

Store in a dark and cool place, not cold. Too much light exposure will produce a toxic green discoloration on the surface. These potatoes should be thrown away. Peeled raw potatoes can be stored in water and a little vinegar for up to 3 days.

Roasted potatoes

For crispy roasted or fried potatoes, first parboil the evenly cut pieces for 15 minutes. Drain well and shake the potatoes in the lidded pot vigorously to rough up the surfaces.

fruit & vegetables

Mashed potato

When making mashed potato, use warm milk to give them a fluffier texture. An alternative to adding milk or butter to potatoes is to just reserve the boiled cooking water and use this to replace the dairy additions, then season to taste. Place a linen towel over the top of a pot of mashed potatoes to absorb excess moisture and keep them fluffy.

Potato preparation

Crispy fried potatoes can be achieved by soaking cleaned and peeled potatoes in cold water first. This will remove excess starch. Pat them dry thoroughly before frying. Potatoes soaked in salt water for 20 minutes before baking will cook more rapidly. Add a little white vinegar or squeeze a little lemon into the water for boiling unpeeled potatoes. This discourages discoloration and helps them keep their shape. Press leftover boiled potatoes into flat pancakes. Individually wrap in plastic wrap and store in the freezer. They can be fried in hot oil or butter without being defrosted.

Waxy versus floury

Waxy potatoes such as white, new, and red-skinned are firm with high moisture and low starch content. Their thin skins can be eaten and digested easier than other varieties. These are used primarily for boiling and sautéing. When cooked, they tend to hold together best. On the other hand, floury potatoes such as the Idaho, sweet, and yam types have thicker skin, less moisture, and high starch content. They are preferred for baking and deep-frying. Once peeled and cooked, the flesh has a sweeter flavor and waxier consistency.

Snapping beans

Avoid fresh green and yellow beans that have discoloration and brown spots. The beans should be firm. To test the freshness, snap the bean in two; it should not bend, rather it should break in two to lightly applied pressure.

Snap frozen

Fresh green and yellow beans may be stored in a sealed plastic bag or container for 3 days. If they are immediately blanched and frozen, they can be stored for up to 1 year.

Brilliant green

The beans will become a brilliant green color if you add some olive oil to the boiling water before adding the beans.

Types of fresh beans

• Fresh beans tend to be more tender and sweeter than dry beans and are also easier to prepare as they do not require soaking before being cooked.

• Green, yellow (wax), snap, and string beans are picked when they are young enough to eat with the pod. Haricot vert (slender French green beans) are desirable for their delicate shape and intense flavor. They also contain many nutrients, such as vitamin C, folate, and iron.

• The pods should snap when broken in half and are noted for their juiciness and crunchy texture. New varieties of string beans often do not require the traditional stripping of strings as the fibrous string has been bred out of the species.

fruit & vegetables

Dried beans

Slow cooking

Dried beans, particularly the larger varieties, require lengthy cooking at a slow simmer. Remember that the older dried beans are, the longer they will take to cook. Next time you are cooking beans, boil enough to freeze for the future.

Leftover ideas

Purée cooked beans with yogurt, sour cream, minced garlic, lemon juice, fresh herbs, and seasoning to make a delicious dip. Leftover beans may also be refrigerated and used within 2 days to boost salads with their heartiness, flavor, and texture.

Easy digestion

Always cook dried beans and peas in fresh water as opposed to the water in which they have been soaking. By adding 3 stalks of celery for every 2 cups of beans, they will be easier to digest. The addition of 1 teaspoon of baking soda to the cooking process will also aid digestion, as will adding a sheet of nori or dried seaweed to the pot. If your bean recipe calls for tomatoes, add them with salt after the beans are completely cooked to avoid toughness.

Snow peas

Crisp and fresh

For a perfectly crisp but cooked texture, pour boiling water into a bowl of snow peas. When the intense green color appears, drain them in a colander, and immediately rinse with cold water.

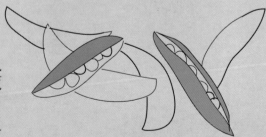

Peas

Pea pods

Select pea pods that are well filled but not bulging. Avoid any that are dried, spotted, yellow, or flabby.

Blanch and freeze

Pea pods can be stored loosely in a container or plastic bag for up to 5 days in the refrigerator. When blanched, briefly and rapidly frozen, they keep well for up to 1 year.

Pea and bacon soup

Serves 4–6

2 tbsp olive oil
2 bay leaves
4 thick slices bacon, coarsely chopped
1 small onion, coarsely chopped

2 potatoes, peeled and diced
4 cups/1 liter water
salt and freshly ground black pepper
3 cups/300 g shelled peas
½ cup/125 g plain yogurt

❶ Heat the oil in a large saucepan. Add the bay leaves, bacon, and onion, and stir well. Cover the pan and cook fairly gently for 10 minutes, stirring occasionally, until the bacon is just cooked and the onion is slightly softened.

❷ Stir in the potatoes, then pour in the water. Season generously and bring to a boil. Reduce the heat, cover the pan, and simmer gently for 30 minutes.

❸ Stir in the peas and bring the soup back to a boil. Then reduce the heat again, cover, and simmer for a further 20 minutes.

❹ Purée the soup in a blender or food processor until smooth. Reheat the soup until just boiling, and taste for seasoning. Remove from the heat and stir in the yogurt, mixing thoroughly until it is fully blended. Serve the soup at once.

Peppers

Preparing peppers

Cut peppers lengthwise into quarters, from stem to bottom. When in four pieces, ease off the stem attachment and discard. Use a small spoon to scoop the whitish core and seeds away.

Red, green, yellow

The bigger the size, the milder the taste: red peppers have a tendency to be sweeter, as do yellow peppers, and the green have a more bitter taste. In selecting peppers to be roasted, choose ones that are unblemished and beginning to wrinkle. These are likely to be mellow in flavor.

Pepper strips

Refrigerate peppers loosely in a tightly sealed plastic bag. To freeze, wash, drain, and cut into strips. Freeze without blanching. Frozen peppers are useful for hot dishes but not for cold salads. Green pepper may change in flavor when frozen in dishes.

Peeled and marinated

To peel peppers, place whole washed peppers on a baking sheet lined with foil or on the open grate of a barbecue. Let the skins blacken evenly with constant turning. When they are predominantly black, place in a glass bowl and cover the top securely with plastic wrap. Let stand 25 minutes. Uncover and rub off the skins. Peeled peppers make a delicious salad when marinated in extra-virgin olive oil, garlic, and herbs.

Roast peppers

2 large green bell peppers, seeded and quartered lengthwise
2 large red bell peppers, seeded and quartered lengthwise
1 tbsp fennel seeds
2 bay leaves
6 tbsp extra virgin olive oil
2 cloves garlic, finely chopped

Serves 4

1 tsp sugar
¼ cup/60 ml sherry vinegar
salt and freshly ground black pepper
zest of 1 lemon, pared off in shreds using a zester
handful of fresh basil sprigs, shredded, to serve
lemon wedges, to serve

❶ Preheat the broiler. Place the pieces of green and red pepper skin sides up on a grill rack and grill for 5–7 minutes until black and softened slightly. Wrap in foil and leave until cold.

❷ Meanwhile, roast the fennel seeds and bay leaves together in a small saucepan until the seeds are aromatic. Shake the pan often and remove it from the heat as soon as the seeds smell. Do not overcook or they will taste bitter. Add the olive oil and garlic to the hot pan, then set it aside to cool.

❸ Whisk the sugar, vinegar, and plenty of seasoning together. Gradually whisk in the oil, adding all the seeds and the bay leaves. Stir in the lemon zest. Skin the pieces of pepper and add them to the dressing, turning each piece and making sure they are well-coated. Cover, and marinate for 24 hours.

❹ To serve, divide the green and red peppers evenly among four plates. Spoon all the flavored oil, seeds, and lemon over them, but discard the bay leaves. Sprinkle with basil and add lemon wedges.

Smooth and shiny

Hotter varieties of peppers are called chiles and are primarily used for flavoring. Look for chiles that are shiny and free of discoloration. The surface should be smooth and free of wrinkles. A rule of thumb is that the smaller the chile, the hotter it is.

Chile powder

To make you own chile powder, roast dried chile peppers on a baking sheet in a 375° F/190° C/Gas 5 oven for 15 minutes. Slice and remove the stems and season. Grind the peppers with a mortar and pestle until fine.

Drying out

Keep chiles fresh in a sealed plastic bag in your vegetable crisper drawer. If you have a large quantity, you may dry them. Dried chiles add wonderful flavor to soups, stews, and sauces. Pierce and sew a loop through them with a clean needle and nylon thread. You may tie the ends of the threads together and make a garland ring. Hang them from a hook or on the wall to air-dry. Dried chiles that turn cloudy or dark red may taste bitter. These should be discarded. Refrigerate those that have maintained their shiny luster for use in cooking.

Frozen heat

Wash and place whole in an airtight plastic bag before freezing. The chiles may be used from frozen. They soften enough for preparation after a few minutes out of the freezer.

Cool down

Reduce the heat of chiles by slicing them lengthwise and scraping out the seeds and membrane with a small paring knife. Use rubber gloves or wash your hands thoroughly after handling chiles. The oils can cause irritation to the skin, but most importantly avoid contact with the eyes. Rinse your eyes immediately with clear water if there is irritation from chile oil.

Dried chiles

Dried chiles range from the reddish-brown ancho, which requires soaking in liquid; to the crushed red pepper for introducing a piquant taste to dishes. Whether using fresh or dried chiles, cooking them will mellow the heat factor. Use all varieties sparingly to discover the level you and your guests find palatable.

fruit & vegetables

Eggplant

Excellent eggplant

The surface should have a shiny or polished appearance. Look for a plump shape, firm feel, and deep violet color.

Brown paper bag

Store eggplant in a paper bag in the refrigerator vegetable crisper drawer. Keeping in plastic can cause decay, indicated by spotting and sliminess on the surface.

Roasted eggplant purée

Bake whole eggplant on a baking sheet in a 275° F/140° C/Gas 1 oven for 45 minutes. Remove from the oven and, while still warm, cut each in half. Scoop out the meat from the shell and purée in the food processor with extra-virgin olive oil and seasoning to taste. You can also roast garlic and shallots along with the eggplant to add to the purée. Serve as a hot vegetable or at room temperature as a dip.

Bitter and oily

Slice the eggplant into rings for baking or grilling. Score a crisscross diamond pattern on the surface of each to ensure even cooking. Set the rings in a colander. To reduce the taste of bitterness and prevent excessive oil absorption, rub a little coarse salt over the surfaces. Rub on lemon juice as well to avoid brown discoloration. Drain for 20 minutes, rinse in cold water, and dry before cooking.

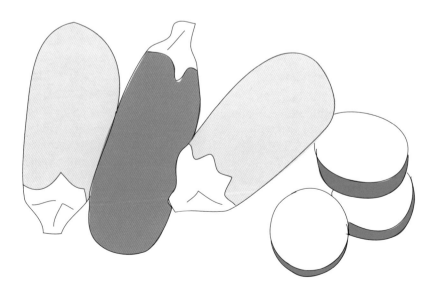

Speedy softening

Winter varieties, such as acorn, butternut, and spaghetti, will be easier to work with when heated briefly in the microwave first. Set the whole squash intact and uncovered into the microwave at the highest setting for 2 minutes cooking. Cut, scoop out the seeds, and follow your recipe for preparation.

Summer and winter

During the summer, squashes can be loosely covered and stored in the refrigerator for up to 3 days. Colder weather allows for storage in a cool, dry place for up to 2 weeks. Once blanched, they can be frozen for up to 1 year.

Cook it up

For more conventional cooking, slice winter squashes in half and scoop out the seeds. Trim the bottom off so it sits flat. Brush the bottom with a little oil to prevent sticking. Add a little butter into the cavity and bake on a baking sheet in a preheated 350° F/180° C/Gas 4 oven for 45 minutes, or until tender. The squash is now ready for additional recipe preparation. Boiling pieces of squash takes about 10 minutes, and a steaming method takes approximately 15 minutes.

Dull not shiny

Acorn and butternut squashes have dull toned skins when ripe; those with shiny skins are not as ripe.

Types of squashes

Squashes fall into two major categories: thin-skinned and thick-skinned. Winter squashes are characterized by thick skin and fibrous flesh. The skin is peeled away before or after cooking, while the seeds are scooped away. Common examples are pumpkin, acorn, butternut, and spaghetti. Winter squash is most frequently baked in slices, but also works well in soup and as an accompaniment to meat dishes in a purée form. Pumpkin is naturally the main ingredient in winter holiday pies and cakes.

The thin-skinned variety is noted for being harvested young, when the entire vegetable can be consumed, raw or cooked. Examples are zucchini, yellow, and patty pan. In addition to their presence in salads and served with dips, they may be sautéed, boiled, baked, stir-fried, and pickled.

fruit & vegetables

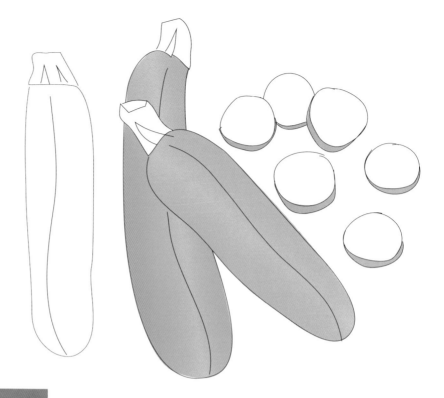

Zucchini

Zucchini green

Look for a clear green color, narrow shape, and supple texture to the touch.

Watery zucchini

Cover loosely in plastic wrap and refrigerate for up to 3 days. Avoid freezing due to the high moisture content.

Freezing vegetables

The success of freezing vegetables is based on blanching them in rapid boiling water first. The amount of time generally ranges between 1 and 5 minutes, depending on the size and density. This process will preserve color, texture, and the nutritional elements, as well as arrest the deterioration process. After blanching the vegetables, dip them in an ice-cold water bath. When they are cool enough to handle, drain and dry them, then seal them in airtight containers, and freeze.

No washing

Do not wash cultivated mushrooms. This will make them soggy, as well as diminish their flavor and nutritional value. Use a mushroom brush or a damp cloth to remove any excess dirt. Cut away only the tip of the stems. Add a little lemon juice when cooking white mushrooms to maintain their white color.

Fry and freeze

Store in a brown paper bag at the bottom of the refrigerator. Do not store in plastic in order to avoid spotting or a slimy consistency. Handle fresh mushrooms with care as they bruise easily. To freeze, first fry the fresh mushrooms in a dry pan at a medium temperature to extract the moisture. Fry until dry. Cool, add a little salt, and freeze in a sealed bag.

Moist mushrooms

The stems and caps should be attached snugly together to characterize freshness. They should be firm and moist with no evidence of damp patches. Common white and tan aroma mushrooms are best when the surface shows no signs of shriveling and an overall color distribution. Avoid dryness at the end of the stem, as this indicates that they may have been stored too long. As common mushrooms mature, the underside of the cap begins to reveal an opening of the gills. Mature open mushrooms have a stronger flavor than small and/or pale, closed cap or button types.

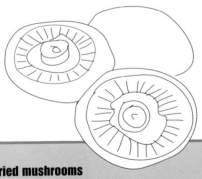

Dried mushrooms

Reconstitute dried mushrooms with boiling water in a glass or ceramic bowl. Fully submerge them and cover the top with a plate for 20 minutes. This will allow them to steam. Retain the excess liquid, strain through a fine mesh colander, and use as a stock for soups or sauces. Create your own soup or stew enhancer by pulverizing your favorite dried mushrooms to a powder and storing in a sealed jar in a dark, cool place.

Corn

Sweet corn

Boil corn in a mixture of half milk and half water to make it tender and sweet. Never add salt to corn while it is cooking to avoid toughness. You may add a little sugar to the liquid for an additional sweetness in flavor. Leftover cut corn can be added to pancake batter to make corncakes.

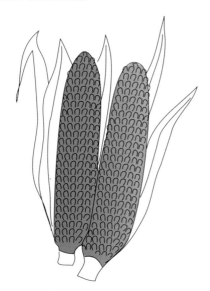

Ginger

Smooth skin

Look for fresh, plump ginger with skin that is not withered, and firm flesh.

Scraping and grating

Fresh ginger can be stored in a glass jar with a seal top in a dry, cool pantry. Scrape the skin off fresh ginger with the edge of a spoon, rather than a knife. There will be less waste. When ginger is frozen, it is much easier to grate.

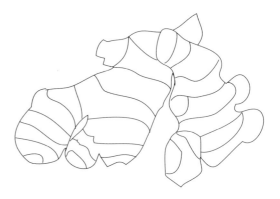

Garlic

Paper skin

The best garlic will have a plump appearance with slightly shiny, papery skin, and no signs of shriveling. The bulb should be quite firm and very tight. Reject bulbs with green shoots at the top. The green shoots within a garlic clove should always be removed before preparation to avoid bitterness in taste.

Olive oil cloves

As with other herbs, garlic should be stored in a dry, cool pantry away from the stove and other heat sources. Peeled garlic gloves, chopped or whole, may be preserved in olive oil in a covered container. If stored in the coldest part of the refrigerator, it will last for 2 weeks.

Roasted garlic

1 whole bulb garlic | olive oil, to drizzle

Serves 1–2 as an appetizer

❶ Begin by selecting the freshest bulb. Slice off the stem from the top of the bulb, revealing the cloves' naked tops.

❷ Drizzle olive oil over the exposed heads and set in a casserole dish with the cut side face up.

❸ In a preheated oven set to 375° F/ 190° C/Gas 5, bake for 30 minutes, or until the cloves are soft to the touch.

❹ While still warm, pinch the cloves out from their papery shell. They are ready to be spread on croutons, used as a component in dips, or served as a garnish for roasts.

Mild and mellow

The flavor becomes more delicate the longer garlic is cooked. Slow cook whole cloves or large slivers for a subtler flavor in soups and stews.

Lay flat

Flatten a whole garlic clove with the skin on. This will loosen the outer covering and make it easy to remove. Cut away the base tip and remove the bitter green shoot, if it exists, in the center. Before you begin chopping garlic, add a little coarse salt to absorb the juice and intensify the flavor.

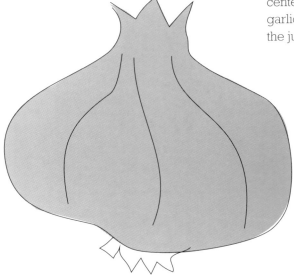

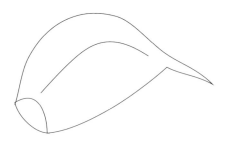

chapter 6

meat poultry & fish

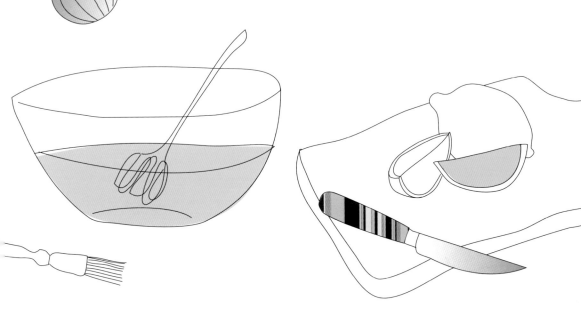

Meat

Under wraps

Transfer meat wrapped in store paper to loose plastic wrap. Meat needs to breathe in order to discourage bacterial growth, and sometimes meat can take on a dried appearance when left in its original packaging. Store in a sealed container in the coldest section of your refrigerator promptly after purchase. You may store it there for up to 2 days, otherwise it should be frozen. The sealed container will deter contamination from the dripping of blood or juices onto other foods and surfaces.

Portion control

Meat is an extremely versatile product and can be frozen when fresh or cooked. High-fat meats can be frozen for up to 6 months. Low-fat meats can be frozen for up to 1 year. Steaks, burgers, and cutlets should be individually wrapped with wax paper or plastic wrap, so that they can be removed individually as required. Divide ground meat into portion sizes, individually wrap in plastic wrap, then press flat. This will economize on space in the freezer and the thin pack of meat will defrost more quickly. To decrease the risk of food poisoning, do not refreeze meat that has thawed (unless it is cooked in a suitable recipe).

Keep it separate

Keep different types of meat in separate containers when storing. If you are storing meat in the refrigerator for a few days, brush the surface with oil to prevent a dry crust.

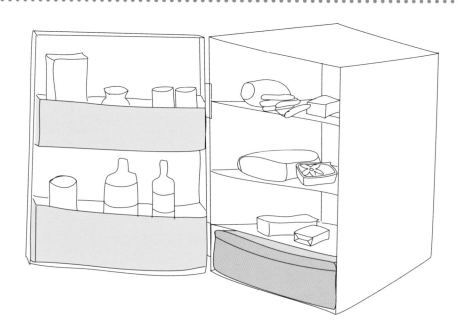

Canned fruit

Reserve the leftover syrup from canned fruits to add to meatloaf or to use as a glaze for baked ham or roast pork.

Preparing liver

Soak beef liver in tomato juice for 3 hours in the refrigerator to tenderize before cooking. To produce a milder flavor, particularly in pork liver, soak it in milk in the refrigerator for 1 hour. Drain and dry on a paper towel.

Salting meat

If you salt meat before cooking, the juices will have a tendency to run out faster and it will take longer to brown. Salt about halfway through the cooking process and add more to taste, at the end of cooking.

Marinating meat

Meat that is on the tough side can be marinated in pineapple juice for 3 hours in the refrigerator. Drain off the juice and dry with a paper towel before cooking.

Prevent curling

Lightly score the edges of chops and steaks with a sharp knife every ½ inch/ 1 cm to prevent the meat from curling during cooking.

Roasting meat

A roast with the bone in will cook faster than a boneless roast because the bone conducts the heat. Leave a roast to stand at room temperature for 1 hour before cooking. Brush with oil before and during the roasting process to seal in the juices.

Sauces
Use very little oil when preparing sauces for red meat. Fat and moisture from the meat during the cooking process provides ample flavor and additional liquid.

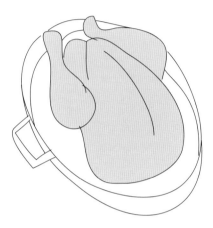

Low-fat broiling

Certain kinds of meats, like ribs and sausages, can be parboiled before broiling to reduce their fat content.

Dicing meat

When dicing meat into cubes for browning and braising, cut them to a uniform size to ensure even cooking.

Casseroles
Both casseroles and soups can be made in larger quantities than required so that there is enough to freeze additional batches. When there isn't time to plan a meal or unexpected guests arrive, simply take the casserole out of the freezer and heat in the oven.

Easy slicing

Meat that has been frozen for 45 minutes is easier to slice thinly into strips with a sharp knife for stir-frying.

Beef and wine casserole

Serves 6

½ cup/55 g all-purpose flour
salt and freshly ground pepper
3 lb/1.5 kg chuck steak or other
stewing beef, cut into 2-in/
5-cm cubes
about 4 tbsp vegetable oil
2 large onions, thinly sliced
1 cup/250 ml fruity red wine
2 cups/500 ml beef stock or water

½ cup/125 ml tomato ketchup
2 cloves garlic, finely chopped
2 bay leaves
1 large bouquet garni (see page 120)
2–3 carrots, cut into ½-in/1-cm pieces
1 lb/450 g butternut or acorn squash,
cut into chunks
10 oz/275 g pearl onions, peeled
1–2 tbsp chopped parsley, to garnish

❶ Put the flour in a plastic bag and season with salt and pepper. Working in small batches, put a few cubes of beef in the bag, twist the bag closed, and shake to coat the meat evenly. Transfer the meat to a plate and continue to coat the remainder.

❷ Heat about 4 tbsp oil over medium-high heat in a large heavy-based saucepan. Working in batches, brown the beef cubes evenly on all sides, about 7 minutes for each batch, until all the beef is browned.

❸ Add a little more oil, if necessary, then add the sliced onions. Cook for about 5 minutes, stirring until softened. If you like a thicker stew, sprinkle over any remaining flour and cook for about 2 minutes, stirring to scrape up any browned bits

from the bottom of the pan. Gradually whisk in the wine, stock, or water, ketchup, garlic, bay leaves, and bouquet garni, and season to taste.

❹ Bring to a boil, skimming off any surface foam. Replace the beef, reduce the heat to medium-low and simmer, covered, for 1½–1¾ hours, stirring occasionally, until the meat is almost tender. After simmering for 1 hour, stir in the carrots; and, after 1¼–1½ hours, stir in the butternut squash.

❺ Remove the bouquet garni from the stew and stir in the pearl onions. Simmer for a further 20 minutes, covered. Sprinkle with parsley and serve immediately.

The color of beef

Choose meat that is a dark red color and marbled with a little fat. Meat that is light red or has a bluish cast and no fat can be chewy. Meat that is a very bright red may not have been aged sufficiently.

Taking it home

Whether the beef is whole or cut into pieces, make sure it is wrapped tightly in plastic wrap. Store in the refrigerator for up to 5 days and freeze for up to 1 year. Ground beef should be treated the same, but refrigerated for no more than 2 days and frozen for up to 2 months.

Ground beef

Ground beef needs quite a lot of fat running through it to prevent it breaking up. Minced steak may be too lean for burgers and meatballs—look instead for a pale, streaky meat.

Burgers

For a juicier hamburger, add ½ cup/125 ml cold water to each pound of meat before grilling. Never press down with your spatula on hamburgers that are cooking. If you do, you lose flavor and texture with the loss of juices.

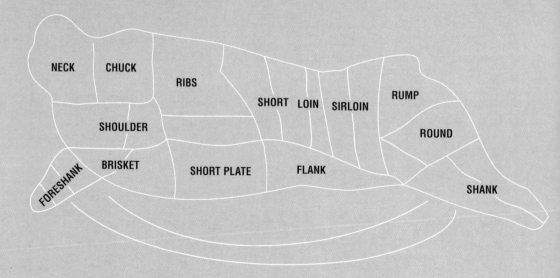

NECK   CHUCK   RIBS   SHORT LOIN SIRLOIN   RUMP

SHOULDER   ROUND

FORESHANK   BRISKET   SHORT PLATE   FLANK   SHANK

Cuts of meat

The forequarters, including cuts such as the neck, chuck, shoulders, and foreshanks of the animal tend to be more sinewy and therefore need slow, moist cooking. These cuts have less fat on them and are more suitable for braising, stewing, and pot-roasting to tenderize them. The ribs are best suited to roasting. The shanks of beef are best served stewed or braised, whilst cuts from the other hindquarter areas, such as the rump, sirloin, short loin, and round can be roasted, or grilled and fried as steaks, as these are often the tenderest, fattiest, and most prime meat parts of the animal.

BBQ Homemade beefburgers

Makes 8

2 tbsp oil
1 onion, finely chopped
1 clove garlic, crushed
2 lb 4 oz/1 kg ground lean beef

1 tsp dried thyme
1 tsp dried parsley
1 tsp Worcestershire sauce
salt and freshly ground black pepper

❶ Heat the oil in a frying pan and cook the onion and garlic for 10 minutes until softened. Let cool.

❷ Place the beef, thyme, parsley, and Worcestershire sauce in a large mixing bowl. Season well with salt and pepper. Stir in the onion and garlic mixture.

❸ Divide the mixture into eight and shape into patties. Place on waxed paper and let chill for 30 minutes.

❹ Grill the beefburgers over very hot coals for 10–15 minutes and serve.

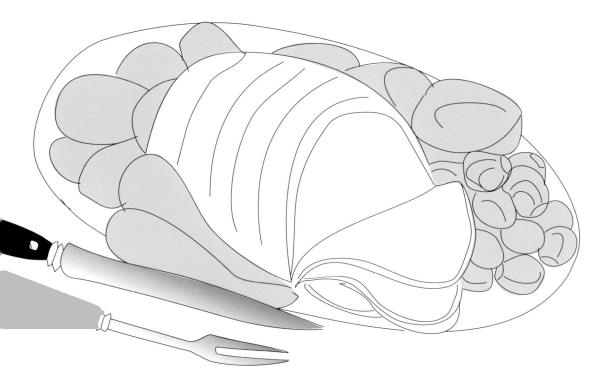

What cut?

Prime cuts of meat have been aged to improve their flavor and texture, while meat for stewing and casseroles is sold younger. When looking for pot-roast meats, try crosscut beef shanks. Pot roasting is a good way of cooking less tender cuts that are best left whole. Consider chuck for stewing meat. It has a high fat content, which bastes the meat and keeps it tender as it is slow-cooked.

Steaks

The best steaks come from the least exercised parts of the animal and have little muscle. Tenderloin or fillet steaks are extremely tender, but can lack flavor. If T-bone and porterhouse steaks are priced the same per pound, choose the porterhouse because it has more tenderloin. Sirloin or New York steaks have a great taste, while rump is perhaps the most flavorful cut of all.

Hanger steak

This cut of beef is a pretty well kept secret. It is sometimes referred to as "butcher's tenderloin" because it is reserved for those in the know. In France, it is called "onglet" and served commonly in bistros. The meat hangs off the kidneys and has a slightly chewy texture with an intense meaty flavor. If available, it can be purchased at a much lower price than tenderloin. Check it out next time at the butcher's shop.

Sausages

Making your own pork sausages means that you can cut down on the amount of fat and do away with the additives used in commercially produced brands. By adding moisture-rich ingredients to your sausagemeat, such as chopped apple, raisins, onions, mushrooms, or even tofu, sausages can retain their moisture, but with less of the fat. Pat cooked sausages dry with a paper towel to reduce fat even further.

Ham

The butt end will always be meatier than the shank end, thus it is more economical to buy. The shank end is usually easier to carve. Both cuts are tender and juicy when prepared properly. Refrigerate fresh ham for up to 4 days and freeze for up to 9 months.

A healthy choice

Pork tenderloin is one of the leanest meats available, being nearly as low in saturated fats as chicken. A small amount of tenderloin can also go a long way because there is so little fat. It is best served in stir-fry dishes.

Ham stock

Makes about 1¼ cups/300 ml

8 cups/2 liters bones and scraps from a cooked ham, along with 1 well-scrubbed and cleaned ham hock
12 cups/3 liters water, with the addition of any leftover juices from the braising process
1 cup/155 g carrot, peeled and roughly chopped
1 cup/155 g roughly chopped onion
½ cup/70 g chopped celery root or 2 roughly cut ribs of celery with leaves
2 cloves garlic, smashed
4 large bay leaves
6 cloves
1 tbsp dried thyme
salt

❶ Break down the bones and scraps to fit inside a large stockpot. Add all the other ingredients except for the salt. The water should cover all the solid matter by at least 2 inches (5 cm).

❷ Keep the cover on the pot slightly askew to allow some steam to escape and bring to the boil. Once at the boil, lower the temperature and simmer for 4 hours.

❸ Add a little salt after 2 hours, and skim the top periodically.

❹ When finished, let stand to cool, then strain thoroughly. You now have enough stock to make a delicious pea and ham soup.

meat, poultry & fish

Bacon

To prevent bacon from crimping and curling, place it in the cold frying pan before cooking. Otherwise you can soak the bacon in cold water for 10 minutes first, or puncture the length of the bacon strips with a few holes. If your recipe calls for bacon pieces, snip the raw bacon into the pieces with scissors right into the frying pan.

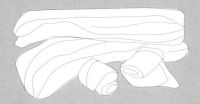

Pink pork

The meat should have a pale pink to pink color. Avoid darker tones, dry flesh, and discolored surfaces. A little marbleizing of fat is good for flavor, however it should be a white or creamy white color. Pork tightly wrapped in plastic wrap may be refrigerated for up to 4 days and frozen for 3 months. Ground pork should be kept only for up to 2 days in the refrigerator, and up to 3 months in the freezer.

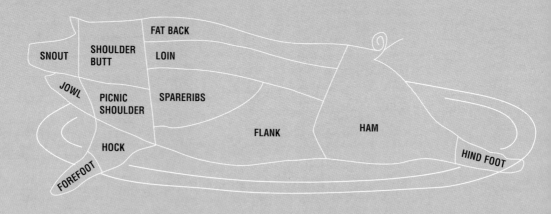

Tough to tender

Braising or stewing are perfect methods of cooking the less tender cuts of pork from the shoulder and leg. Like most stewed dishes, pork prepared in this way often tastes better the next day, when the flavors have had time to develop.

Tangy barbecue pork

Makes about 1¼ cups/300 ml

½ cup/175 g tomato paste
1 tsp Dijon mustard
½ cup/55 g soft brown sugar
1 teaspoon salt
½ tsp chili powder
1 tbsp Worcestershire sauce

1 medium onion, minced
¼ cup/60 ml apple cider vinegar
½ freshly squeezed lemon, juice only
freshly ground black pepper
leftover pork roast, sliced

❶ Combine all the ingredients except the pork together in a saucepan. Stir continuously until it comes to the boil.

❷ Remove from the heat and add the sliced pork roast.

❸ Let stand at room temperature for 30 minutes to marry the flavors. Heat up and serve as a sandwich on warm, crusty French rolls or baguette.

Lamb

How old?

Select lamb with white fat and generous marbling. Avoid meat with fat that is slightly. The darker the red flesh, the older the animal was when slaughtered, and the older the animal, the stronger the taste of the meat. Most lamb on the market is spring lamb, which is slaughtered between 3 and 9 months of age and usually gives a more tender meat. Look for a light pink color. A good way to judge age is through weight.

Lamb cuts

Possibly the most popular cut is the leg, providing generous amounts of lean meat, perfect for roasting or barbecuing. The shank is desirable from a young and lean animal. Braising is a popular method of cooking this part. The rack of lamb or upper ribs may be roasted or grilled whole, or in a crown formation. When singularly or double cut, they become individual chops. The tenderloin is the most tender, lean, and expensive of cuts. It may be roasted or grilled whole, but be sure not to overcook it.

Lamb and chickpea curry

Serves 4

2 tbsp vegetable oil
1 onion, chopped
1-in/2.5-cm piece fresh ginger, finely grated
1 clove garlic, chopped
1 medium tomato, peeled and roughly chopped
1 tsp ground cilantro
2 tbsp curry paste (mild, medium or hot, to taste)

$\frac{2}{3}$ cup/150 ml vegetable or meat stock or water
14-oz/400-g can chickpeas, drained and rinsed
1½ cups/100 g button mushrooms
2 cups/250 g leftover roast lamb, roughly chopped
5 tbsp Greek yogurt
3 tbsp fresh cilantro, chopped
salt and freshly ground black pepper

❶ Heat 1 tablespoon of the oil in a medium saucepan. Add the onion, ginger, and garlic and cook for about 5 minutes until softened. Transfer to a blender or food processor along with the tomato. Process until fairly smooth.

❷ Return to the pan along with the cilantro, curry paste, stock, and chickpeas. Cover and simmer for 20 minutes.

❸ Meanwhile, heat the rest of the oil in a frying pan and add the mushrooms. Cook over a high heat for 5 minutes until golden.

❹ Add the mushrooms with the meat to the chickpea mixture and simmer for 5 minutes. Remove from the heat and let stand for 1–2 minutes. Add the yogurt and cilantro. Season to taste and serve with basmati rice.

A tight wrap

Whole or cut pieces of lamb may be refrigerated with tight plastic wrap packaging for up to 4 days. The same pieces have a freezer life of 9 months. Snugly wrapped ground lamb may be refrigerated for up to 2 days and frozen for up to 3 months.

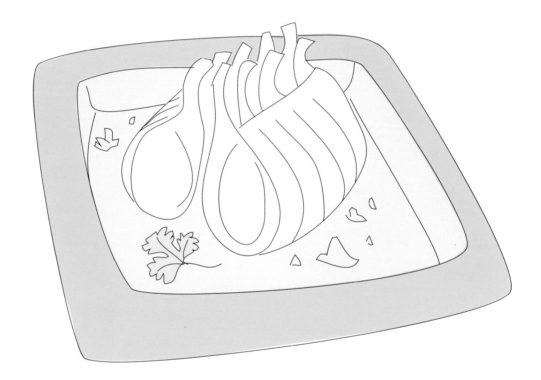

Veal

Keeping it cold

Well-sealed roasts wrapped in plastic wrap may be refrigerated for up to 3 days and frozen for up to 6 months. Ground veal has a shelf life of 2 days in the refrigerator and 3 months in the freezer.

What color?

The meat should be supple to the touch rather than soft or spongy. It should be light pink in color with a smooth grain. Fat should be sparse, and shiny membrane or connective tissue should be absent for the most part. Bones should be white to pink in color.

Poultry

Super clean
Rinse the bird thoroughly in running cold water and pat dry with paper towel. Be sure to clean well inside the cavity and remove any loose or hanging bits. Arrest bacterial growth before you cook poultry by rubbing white distilled vinegar over the entire bird. Use about 2 tablespoons for each 5-pound/2.5-kg bird.

What to look for
Check that the skin of the bird is light-colored. Yellow skin is found on some corn-fed birds. The breast should be full and plump, particularly in the case of turkey. Free-range birds are usually preferable and correspondingly more expensive. Generally there is a higher proportion of fat between the flesh and skin and the meat often feels firmer.

Freezing the bird
When freezing an entire bird, remove any excess fat from the vent end and all the internal organs in the cavity. The leaner the bird, the longer the frozen state can be extended. For best results, place poultry in a self-sealing freezer bag, then wrap it with an outer layer of aluminum foil. This will inhibit freezer burn. Remember to always defrost raw poultry in the refrigerator, allowing 2 hours for each 1 lb/500 g weight of the whole bird.

Chicken

Picking a good one
Select whole chickens that have moist skin and a light, uniform color with no dark patches. The breast should be plump and the smell should be fresh or next to non-existent.

Looking after it
Fresh chicken can be stored for 2 days in the refrigerator and may be stored for up to 3 months in the freezer.

Turning chicken
Never turn chicken over more than once while sautéing or grilling. Peek at the underside by using tongs or a spatula to check doneness.

Extra flavor

The flavor is enhanced if chicken is seasoned and stored for 24 hours in the refrigerator before cooking. Rub chicken parts with spices and herbs and marinate before cooking for even more flavor.

Intensify the experience

If you are stewing chicken ready to dice the meat for casseroles or salads, let it cool in the broth before cutting it into pieces. This will enhance the flavor of the meat and keep it moist.

Southern-fried chicken

Serves 6

1½ cups/350 ml buttermilk
2 tsp salt, half for the buttermilk, and half for the seasoned flour
cayenne pepper, to taste
freshly ground black pepper, to taste

8 boneless, skinless chicken breast halves or other pieces
1½ cups/175g all-purpose flour
vegetable shortening for frying

❶ In a shallow dish, combine the buttermilk, salt, ½ teaspoon cayenne pepper, and black pepper. Add the chicken, coating each piece evenly; cover and chill between 2 and 24 hours, turning once. Drain before using.

❷ Put the flour, salt, cayenne pepper, and black pepper in a plastic freezer bag; close the bag and shake to mix. Drop 2 or 3 pieces of the drained chicken into the bag, and shake gently

to coat evenly. Shake off any excess flour and place the pieces on a wire rack. Repeat with the remaining pieces.

❸ Add enough shortening to create a depth of ½ inch/1 cm in a 10- or 12-inch/25- or 30- cm cast-iron skillet. Heat to 350° F/ 180° C/Gas 4 Carefully lower the chicken pieces into the hot fat, skin-side down. Cover and cook until crisp and golden all over, about 10 minutes. Drain on a wire rack.

Chicken stock

To make chicken stock, take any leftover bones, meat trimmings, and discarded raw vegetable parts, and store them in individually marked and dated containers. Cover with water and seal tightly to prevent freezer

burn. Place them in the freezer and when you are ready to make a stock, empty the contents of the appropriate bag into boiling water. Add additional stock ingredients and discard all solid contents when finished.

meat, poultry & fish

The whole bird

Select a free-range bird for roasting for a notable improvement on standard supermarket offerings. Buy fresh rather than frozen, and hen rather than male birds. Hens are noted for their larger and more tender breasts. Keep turkey for up to 4 days in the refrigerator and up to 6 months in the freezer.

Perfect gravy

Never drain off the brown bits and sticky residue left in the roasting pan, as these are the essence of a perfect gravy. Make the gravy in the pan in which the turkey was cooked. Be sure to keep the bird warm in a low oven, or place it back to the pan to be heated through in the sauce for a few minutes once you are satisfied with the flavor of the gravy.

A perfect roast

Roast in a 350° F/180° C/Gas 4 oven for 18 minutes for each 1 lb/500 g from 10 to 14 lb/5 to 7 kg in weight, and 16 minutes per 1 lb/500 g for birds over 14 lb/7 kg in weight. Turkeys are ideal for stuffing, but only stuff the bird just prior to roasting it, as the moisture provides the perfect environment for bacteria to breed. As the bird roasts, note whether the juices or fat begin to scorch. If necessary, add a little stock or water. If the turkey has been trussed during roasting, remove the string once it has been taken out of the oven. Loosely cover the top of the bird with aluminum foil and leave to rest on a rack for 15 minutes. This redistributes the juices prior to carving and makes for easier slicing. To test for doneness, prick the thigh of the bird with a sharp fork. If the juice runs clear, the bird is done.

Turkey—how to carve it

Once the turkey has rested, transfer it to a cutting board that has a surrounding moat. This will collect precious running juices. Slice through the crispy skin connecting the breast and the thigh. A fork should serve to keep the turkey steady. Carve downward to where the thigh is attached, including the meat along the back. Bend the thigh away from the breast, followed by slicing through the joint that separates the leg. If you twist your knife away from you, the leg should dislodge. Slice horizontally above the wings to accommodate easy slicing of the breast meat. Leave the wings slightly attached for steadying support. Holding the fork against the breastbone, carve layers on the bias to the desired thickness

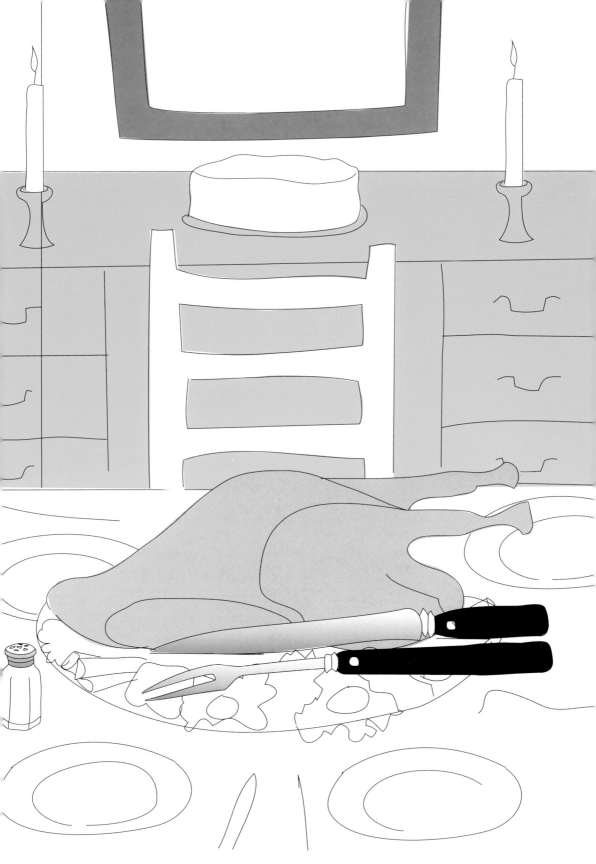

Which duck?

Select a female duck for juicier meat. The fat should be white, not yellow.

Scoring the skin

Score the skin side of a duck breast in a crisscross fashion to ensure even cooking of the meat and prevent curling. This will allow excess fat to release and assist in the browning process.

Dark meat

Unlike other poultry, ducks are made up of entirely dark meat, however, a duck's breast is very tender and lean, whilst its legs are firm and tough. Cook these parts separately for best results.

Good fat!

Duck and goose fat is very good for frying other foods, particularly potatoes. Prick the skin of the bird, especially at the breast area taking care not to pierce the flesh as this will result in the loss of other juices. The bird's fat will be released into the roasting pan. It will store for weeks in the refrigerator and months in the freezer.

Duck roast

To remove excess fat, put a whole apple in the cavity of a duckling before roasting. After cooking, reserve the duck fat and store in a sealed jar in the refrigerator to use later.

kitchen genius

Duck a l'orange

Serves 4

2 large duck breasts
1 shallot, chopped
1 clove garlic, chopped
1 tbsp fresh thyme leaves
2 tbsp Cointreau or
orange-flavored liqueur

2 tbsp port
¼ cup/50 ml chicken stock
1 orange, finely grated zest
   and juice
2 tbsp orange marmalade
salt and freshly ground black pepper

❶ To prepare the duck breasts, lightly score the skin at ½-in/1-cm intervals. Now turn the duck breasts and repeat to give a diamond pattern. Be careful not to cut the flesh. These cuts will allow the fat to escape.

❷ Heat a large frying pan over a medium-high heat. When hot, add the duck breasts, skin-side-down. Reduce the heat to medium and cook for about 7–8 minutes until well browned. Turn and cook for a further 3–4 minutes. Remove from the pan.

❸ Remove as much fat as possible from the pan with a metal

spoon, leaving about 1 tablespoon only. Return the pan to a medium heat and add the shallot. Cook for 3–4 minutes until softened, then add the garlic and thyme. Cook for a further 1 minute before adding the Cointreau and port. Simmer until reduced by half. Add the chicken stock, orange juice, and zest and bring to the boil. Simmer until reduced by half. Stir in the marmalade until melted. Season to taste.

❹ Slice the duck breasts thickly and serve immediately with the sauce.

Fish and shellfish

What to buy?

Some of the most popular fish consumed is of the firm, meaty variety. It is quite easy to purchase cod, halibut, sea bass, and salmon, in fillet or steak form. Always attempt to purchase these cuts where prepared on the spot. This reduces the degree of deterioration since it minimizes the amount of time that the fish is exposed to bacteria. The darker the fish flesh, the higher the calories.

Types of cut

Although it's probably best to buy your fish whole in order to really gauge its freshness, fish is also sold in many different cuts. The most common and simple to prepare being steaks, fillets, medallions, and chunks. Cleaning and filleting a whole fish can be a very time-consuming task.

Is it fresh?

In choosing fresh fish, you have to trust all five senses. First ask if the fish is fresh.

- Fish should smell fresh.
- Ocean fish should have the slightest hint of sea and salt.
- All fish should feel firm and supple.
- Scales should be shiny and skin translucent.
- Eyes should protrude clear and bright. Avoid bloodshot and filmy eyes.
- Gills should have a deep red cast.
- Test for freshness at home by putting the fish in a large bowl of cold water. If it floats, it is fresh.

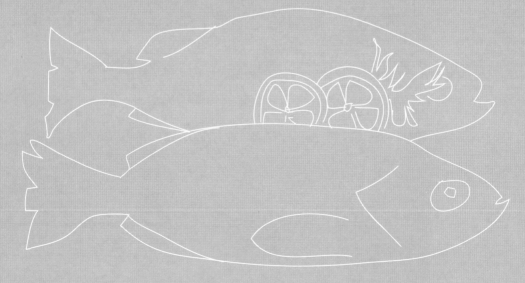

Fresh tricks

For best results in the refrigerator, store fish in tightly wrapped plastic wrap and on ice, with the ability for the water to drain. It is best to refrigerate fresh fish for no more than 1 day, however, fresh, rinsed, and gutted fish will keep for up to 3 days in the refrigerator if you rub with coarse salt and pack it in a towel dampened with sugar and vinegar. Rinse fish with cold water and pat dry before using.

Fish freezing

Both fresh and prepared fish may be frozen, although home freezers have a tendency to chill more slowly than commercial ones. This results in the formulation of ice crystals, which can damage texture and flavor. Lower-fat fish freezes best. This includes cod, pike, and pollock. Firm fish fillets or steaks, like salmon and tuna, also freeze well. They may be stored from 6 to 8 months. Oilier fish, such as mackerel and halibut may be stored from 3 to 4 months.

Prolong freezing

To prolong the freezer life of fish, remove fillets that have been frozen within 48 hours. They may be dipped in cold water, wrapped, labeled, and returned to the freezer. This process, called glazing, will double their life in the freezer. Always defrost fish in the refrigerator before preparation in order to minimize damage to texture and moisture loss.

Fishy hint
If the fresh fish feels at all slimy, prepare a bath of 1 tablespoon sea salt to 8 cups/2 liters cold water. Add a few trays of ice cubes to plummet the temperature. Submerge the fish and let it soak for 15 minutes. Remove and pat dry. The scent should be sea fresh and the texture or feel, slime-free.

meat, poultry & fish

Fish filleting

If you generally use your right hand, filleting a whole fish begins by positioning the head on the right and the tail on the left. Most often you begin by taking a knife and removing the head just to the right of the gills. Make a cut to the left just under the gills. Slide the knife to the left along the center seam, which is positioned above the central bone of the fish. Next remove the dorsal, or top fin away from the central portion of the fish in a right-to-left fashion. Follow the slightly indented seam that separates the fleshier part of the main body to this thinner portion. Repeat this movement with the anal, or bottom fin. This last segment contains the roe if you are interested in the delicacy. Removing the flesh from the myriad of tiny bones in these two segments is more work, and can be reserved for later. Return to the central portion of the fish. Slide your knife under each divided fillet and push away from the central bone. When this is completed, you should be able to lift the entire bone, with tail intact, from the bottom fillets. Just slide your knife under the bone from left to right, lift it gradually, being careful to separate it from the meat, and discard.

Descaling fish

Scale fish under cold running water, or by rubbing distilled white vinegar over the surface first. Salt your fingertips and the cutting surface to get a good grip on the fish. Scrape the scales off with a sharp-edged spoon, working from the tail towards the head. Rub coarse salt into the cavity of a whole fish to remove any lingering residue, then rinse thoroughly in cold water prior to cooking. Before serving cooked sides of fish, check for bones and remove with flat-end tweezers. Run your fingers gently over the top to make sure you have extracted the bones.

Breadcrumb coating

This batter is commonly used to make fried fish. Take two bowls and two separate forks. Whisk whole eggs into one bowl. Mix breadcrumbs and seasoning in the other. Dip each fish fillet in the egg wash using the first fork. Hold it over the bath for 20 seconds, allowing the excess egg to run off. Set the fish in the bread-crumb mixture. Roll the fish around so that the surface is entirely covered. Remove it with the second fork. Set the fillet on a rack for 20 minutes before frying. This allows the air to circulate around each fillet and dry the batter. Be sure to use plenty of breadcrumb mixture and remove any clumps, which may be created from excess moisture.

Fish stock

When making fish stock, remove scum after it is brought to the boil the first time.

Flaky fish

Fish is ready when it almost begins to flake. If it flakes, it's overcooked.

Frying fish

Combine flour, seasonings, and salt in a plastic bag. Leave the fish in the flour mixture for 10 minutes before frying.

Boiling fish

When fish is being boiled, add a little milk or lemon juice to the water to maintain its white color.

Grilled fish

Rub lemon juice over the surface of the fish for baking and grilling. This will enhance the flavor and maintain a good color.

Cooking fish fillets and steaks

Salmon or tuna fillets and steaks may be sautéed on top of the stove for 3–5 minutes on each side. The length of time will depend on the temperature you prefer inside. Poach salmon for 10–15 minutes in court bouillon or fish stock. Bake fillets and steaks wrapped in aluminum foil or covered with parchment paper in a preheated 350° F/180° C/Gas 4 oven for 14–18 minutes. Broil marinated salmon for 3–5 minutes on each side. Increase cooking times, based on the same principle, with denser fish such as shark and tuna.

Homemade tartare sauce

Makes 1¼ cups/300 ml

1 quantity of mayonnaise (see right)
1 tsp Dijon mustard
1 tsp finely chopped green olives
**1 tsp finely chopped gherkins
  or cornichons**
1 tsp finely chopped capers
1 tsp chopped fresh parsley
**1 tsp chopped fresh chives
  or tarragon**
**salt and freshly ground black
  pepper**

❶ Mix all the ingredients together until well blended. This sauce is particularly good with deep-fried and crispy breaded fish.

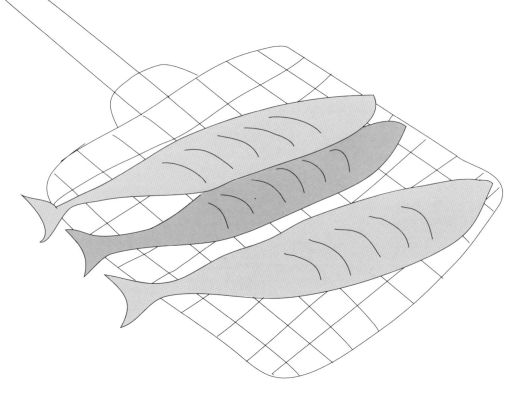

Marinating fish

Soaking fish in a marinade for 20 minutes before cooking really adds to the flavor. If the leftover marinade is going to be added to the final dish, be sure to boil it in the sauce or by itself first for at least 5 minutes to cook out any bacteria.

Barbecuing fish

Before barbecuing fish, ensure that the grill is clean and be sparing when coating the fish with oil, as too much could cause flare-ups. The strong heat chars and flavors the fish surface well, so it is not always necessary to marinate fish first.

Homemade mayonnaise

Makes 1¼ cups/300 ml

1 egg yolk
1 tsp wholegrain mustard
1 tbsp lemon juice

salt and freshly ground black pepper
1 cup/250 ml light olive oil

❶ Put the yolk, mustard, lemon juice, and seasoning into a food processor. Blend for 30 seconds until frothy.

❷ Begin adding the olive oil, drop by drop, until the mixture starts to thicken. Continue adding the oil in a slow,

steady stream until all the oil has been incorporated.

❸ Taste for seasoning, adding a little more lemon juice if necessary. Thin with a little hot water if the mayonnaise is too thick. Refrigerate until needed.

meat, poultry & fish

Pan-fried salmon

Serves 2

2 salmon fillets
salt and freshly ground black pepper

dried herbs, to season
extra virgin olive oil

❶ Try pan-searing salmon. You'll need a super oven-safe pan. Make sure that the salmon fillet is at room temperature. Towel-dry any excess moisture on the flesh, then season with salt, pepper, and your choice of dried herbs. Preheat the oven to the hottest heat possible.

❷ Heat your pan with a coating of extra-virgin olive oil on a medium-high burner. A faint smoke haze means that

it's time to pick up your tongs and set the salmon fillet in the pan. Do not release the fish until the skin is hot enough that it can slide easily on the surface of the oil.

❸ When the skin is crispy, simply flip the fillet over and place the pan in the oven. Wait 3 minutes before removing your supper from the inferno, a perfect medium rare.

An "r" in the month

Do not choose oysters with shells that are open. Traditionally in the Northern Hemisphere, oysters aren't consumed in months without an "r." Once the oyster has been freshly opened, the muscle should react to the touch of a knife or by dripping some lemon juice on it. It should smell very fresh, and of the sea and nothing else. When in doubt, throw it out.

Weigh them down

Once you have brought oysters or other shellfish, like clams or mussels, home, it is best to keep them tightly compacted in a mesh or perforated plastic bag. Set them in a container in the coldest part of the refrigerator, firmly weighted down. This should prolong their life for an extra 2 days, prevent loss of juices, and contribute to the maintenance of their quality.

Easy shucking

After purchasing fresh oysters or other shellfish in the shell, if you can store them in the freezer for 30 minutes they will be easier to shuck.

Can opener oysters

If you don't have an oyster knife, you can use a pointed tip can opener. Place a napkin or towel in the palm of your hand, followed by the oyster with the flat end facing up. Hold the shell firmly and insert the pointed end of the opener between the hinged sides close to the back. Push down firmly on the opener, keeping the shell level so as not to lose the juices. When you can put your fingers between the crack, open with your hands. Cut and loosen the oyster meat from the shell with a knife and serve.

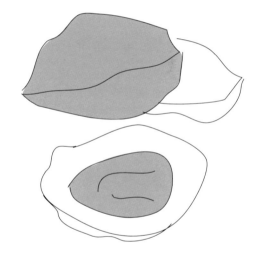

In the refrigerator

Raw shrimp with their shells intact can be refrigerated in a tightly sealed container or plastic bag for up to 2 days. The same holds true for cooked shrimp, with or without the shell.

Deveining

If your recipe calls for shrimp cooked in its shell, take some scissors and snip the shell down the back from the head to the tail. Use a paring knife to remove the black vein, beginning at the base of the head and firmly pulling the strand out all the way to the tail.

Spicy shrimp

Before sautéing, dust the shrimp with spices, such as chili or curry powder. When cooking shrimp, note their shape for doneness. They will contract into a semicircle when they are ready. If they are tightly coiled, they are overcooked. After the shellfish is cooked, balance flavors with a little salt and sugar to taste.

Lime shrimp

Serves 4

24 large raw shrimp
freshly squeezed lime juice

❶ Peel and devein the shrimp. Brush lightly with lime juice.

❸ Cook on a preheated, lightly oiled chargrill pan for 2-3 minutes each side, or until cooked through.

Iced shrimp

Fresh shrimp can be stored in the freezer for up to 6 months in plastic containers filled with cold water. Cooked shrimp, with or without the shell, can be stored for up to 2 months in the freezer. When you are ready to use them, thaw the shrimp in cold running water. When cooked, they should taste fresh.

Sweet scent

Whether you are buying fresh shrimp raw or cooked, with or without the shell, the scent should be sweet and the texture should be firm and moist.

Squid

Fresh or frozen

Whether the squid is purchased clean, raw, or cooked, it will keep for up to 2 days in the refrigerator. Squid stands up to freezing well and it may be purchased cleaned and in a frozen state. Store it in the freezer for up to 3 months.

Quick cooking

The rule for cooking squid is either rapidly over high heat, or long and slow cooking over even heat. The first applies to techniques like deep-frying, which takes approximately 4 minutes, and poaching in court bouillon for roughly 7 minutes. These methods serve best when preparing cleaned baby squid. The latter may also be applied to cleaned older squid. Cut them into pieces and add to a stew, which may be braised for up to 1 hour.

Creamy white

Fresh squid reveals a creamy white color alongside purple skin. If any sign of pink or brown appears on the white surface, avoid it. Look for shiny skin and a fresh sea fragrance. Baby squid is by far the sweetest and most tender. Try to buy whole squid, which includes the delicious tentacles.

Presentation

Before frying or boiling squid, cut a few grooves into the pieces of meat before cooking. The squid will curl up during cooking and look more attractive when served.

meat, poultry & fish

173

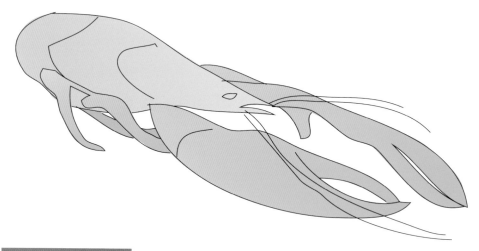

Lobster

Alive and kicking

If buying live lobster, make sure that there is clear evidence that it is alive. It should move with great determination. When selecting a cooked lobster, look for a plump tail that appears to be slightly curled under. This indicates that the lobster was cooked when alive. The female generally has a wider tail and the benefit of the caviar, which is a savory treat in itself.

In and out of the shell

Live lobsters should be stored for no longer than 1 day in water and in a cool place. If it is cooked, with or without its shell, it can be kept for up to 2 days in the refrigerator. Once frozen, lobster has a shelf life of 6 months in the shell and 2 months out of the shell, in a tightly sealed container or plastic bag.

Cutting them open

Use scissors or poultry shears to cut lobster and large crayfish shells lengthwise in half effectively.

Broiled lobster tails

2 whole lobster tails
½ cup/125 g butter, melted
½ tsp ground paprika

Serves 2

salt and freshly ground white pepper, to taste
1 lemon, cut into wedges, to garnish

❶ Preheat the broiler. Put lobster tails on baking sheet. Cut top side of shells lengthwise. Pull shells apart slightly and season meat with butter, paprika, salt, and pepper in equal amounts.

❷ Broil the tails for 5–10 minutes, or until the butter is melted and lightly browned, and the meat is opaque.

Crabmeat

Live crab may be stored in a cool place for up to 2 days. Once it is removed from the shell, it can be stored in the refrigerator for up to 3 days. Vacuum-packed crabmeat that has been pasteurized can be stored for about 2 weeks in the refrigerator, but the taste will not be as intense as that of the fresh crab.

Freezing crabs

Both the pasteurized vacuum-packed variety and fresh crabmeat out of the shell will keep well for up to 1 month in the freezer.

Cracking them open

Wrap crab claws in a dishtowel and set them on a cutting board. Use a hammer to crack the shells before serving.

Cooked crab

Like lobster, buy crab that is still kicking.
If buying cooked crab, remember that it should smell sweet and feel heavy. The females tend to be a bit larger, with a broader expanse of the shell under the body: this contains the coral roe.

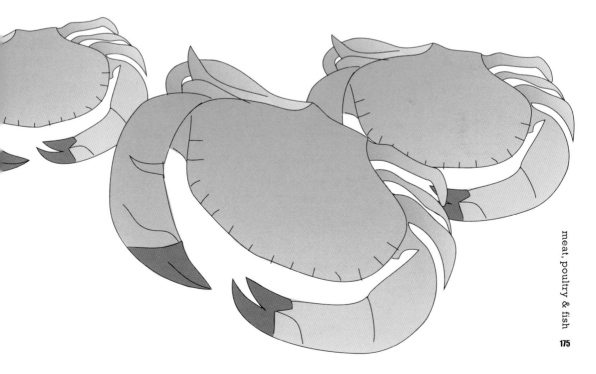

bakery & dairy

Bread

Types of breads

Breads fall into two basic categories: those made with yeast, when the dough goes through a rising or proving process, and quick breads made without yeast, but using a chemical raising agent, like baking powder or baking soda. Yeast breads include the common white Pullman, baguette, and brioche. Sour dough is made from a fermenting batch of starter dough instead of added yeast. Breads without yeast include flatbreads, cornbread, soda bread, and scones. Breads made with whole grains and without additives or a high sugar content are easier for the digestive system to process and help in the ongoing battle with weight problems.

Freezing bagels

If you are planning on keeping bagels any longer than 3 days it is best to freeze them in a plastic bag as soon as you buy them. If you intend to toast your bagels, or use them for sandwiches, slice them before freezing. It is very difficult, not to mention dangerous, to slice a frozen bagel.

Bread crumbs

To make browned bread crumbs from fresh bread:

• Place sliced bread directly onto the racks in a hot oven.

• Place a pan at the bottom of the oven to collect any falling crumbs. Leave the door open slightly to allow air to circulate. Bake the bread slices in the oven until they are dry, crisp, and golden brown.

• Take the bread out to cool.

• Use a food processor, or crush the bread with a rolling pin, to make crumbs. The crumbs may be used for meatballs, batters, or baked goods.

• Store in a sealed plastic bag or container in a cool place.

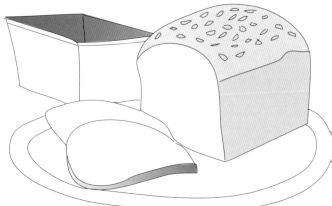

Welsh rarebit

Serves 4

8 oz/225 g sharp Cheddar cheese, grated
1 tsp cornstarch
½ tsp dry mustard
½ cup/125 ml beer

1 tsp Worcestershire sauce
freshly ground black pepper, to taste
1 egg yolk
4 thick slices multi-grain bread, toasted

1. Toss the cheese, cornstarch, and mustard in a mixing bowl.

2. Combine the beer, Worcestershire sauce, and pepper in a medium saucepan. Cook over medium heat, stirring, 2 minutes.

3. Whisk in the cheese mixture and continue to cook, stirring, 2 minutes.

4. Whisk in the egg yolk. Cook for 2 minutes, stirring. Spoon over toasted bread and serve warm.

Bread storage

Plain, crusty breads are stored differently from soft, enriched breads. If you want to preserve the crisp crust, store bread in paper: it will become stale within a day and is best eaten on the same day it is made. If you want to preserve bread for more than a day, wrap the loaves tightly in plastic wrap to prevent any air from getting to them. Then, either freeze or place them in a cool, dark place. Home-made nut breads taste better if they are stored for 24 hours before they are served.

Toaster tip

Consider buying a toaster with a frozen bread setting, as this defrosts bread before toasting it.

Defrosting bagels

Frozen bagels are best left to thaw in a plastic bag at room temperature. Be careful if you use a microwave to thaw your bagels—microwaves cook from the inside out and can dry the center. A very short time (10 seconds) will be enough. If the bagels are being toasted, put them into the toaster frozen—by the time they are toasted, they will be defrosted too!

bakery & dairy

Croutons

Rough cut or slice uniform cubes of dried bread. Gently sauté them in butter, minced garlic, and finely chopped parsley. Cool and serve as a garnish for soups or salads.

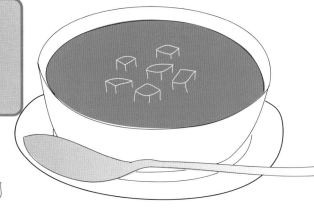

Stuffing

Slightly stale, dry bread makes great stuffing. Combine the bread crumbs with sautéed onions, sage, and thyme, mixed with melted butter and stock.

Toasterbags

Black plastic reusable toasterbags are a quick, clean, and convenient invention to turn your toaster into a toasted sandwich maker.

Freezer fresh

Bread becomes stale quicker in the refrigerator, but it does not turn mouldy as quickly. When storing bread in a tin, add some celery or a carrot. When storing bread in plastic, add a whole peeled potato. Bread with very little fat will keep in the freezer for up to 1 year. Slice and pack securely in a plastic bag with all the air squeezed out. Take out only what you will use immediately.

Frozen bread crumbs

Grind stale baguette or white bread in the food processor. Put the bread crumbs in a plastic bag and store in the freezer. Remove small quantities as required.

Baking your bread

When baking bread, place a small pan of water beside it in the oven to create steam and give the bread a crisp crust.

Bread and butter pudding

Serves 6

⅓ cup/40 g yellow or dark raisins
¾ cup/75 g lightly salted butter, melted
1 lb/450 g stale white bread, cut into approximately 3-inch/ 8-cm cubes
1 lemon, zest only, finely chopped

¼ tsp freshly ground nutmeg
1 tsp powdered cinnamon
½ tsp pure vanilla extract
½ cup/100 g white sugar
2 eggs
2 cups/500 ml whole milk

❶ Mix the raisins, butter, and bread in a bowl until the butter is absorbed.

❷ Add all the other ingredients and stir until evenly combined, keeping the bread pieces whole.

❸ Empty the contents into a greased ovenproof baking dish. Let it stand for 20 minutes.

❹ Mix again and bake in a preheated 325° F/170° C/Gas 3 oven for about 45 minutes, until the pudding is set and golden brown. Serve warm.

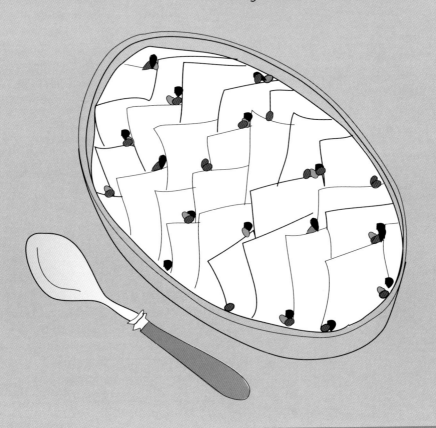

Home-made bread

You will get a finer texture to your bread when you use milk, while water in a recipe will produce coarser bread. Use a clear or translucent container with straight sides to raise your dough. Mark the level at which the dough begins. Measure the distance with a ruler to check the level to which the dough should rise. Rub a little butter or splash your hands in water before working with bread dough. This prevents it from sticking and makes kneading easier.

Examples of quick breads

apple loaf
fruit loaf
pesto bread
pumpkin
  bread
raisin bread
savory
  corn-bread

scones
soda bread
sweet
  breads
naan bread

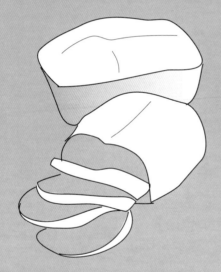

Quick breads

Quick breads are breads that use baking soda and/or baking powder as a leavening agent rather than yeast, so they rise in the oven and do not have to be proved, or allowed to rise, before they are baked. Quick bread recipes usually include few ingredients, can be mixed by hand in a bowl, and made from start to finish in around an hour.

Reviving stale bread

Dry, stale bread is easily revived. If it is a whole loaf, sprinkle a little water on the top and place in the oven until warm. The same technique works with whole baguettes and rolls, but these must be wrapped in aluminum foil. Thick-sliced toast, garlic bread, or bread crumbs are perfectly good made with dry bread.

Club sandwich

To construct the perfect club sandwich, layer cold cooked chicken, turkey, and bacon with lettuce leaves and tomato and pineapple slices between three large buttered square slices of toasted bread. Season with salt and freshly ground black pepper to taste.

Cakes

Freezing cakes

Freshly cooked and cooled cakes freeze very well if they are sealed securely both in plastic wrap and an outer layer of polythene or aluminum foil. Wrapping a cake properly keeps it moist and prevents it from absorbing the flavors or odors of the other food in the freezer. If the cake is frosted, freeze it unwrapped for about 1 hour, until firm, before wrapping as instructed and returning to the freezer.

Chocolate cake

When baking a chocolate cake, use cocoa powder instead of flour to dust the pan. This prevents the white flour "dust" from clinging to the sides of the cake.

bakery & dairy

Chocolate chip muffins

Makes 15

3 cups/375 g all-purpose flour
2 tbsp baking powder
pinch of salt
6 tbsp sugar
⅔ cup/125 g semisweet chocolate chips

¼ cup/50 g butter
6 squares/175 g semisweet chocolate, cut up
2 eggs, beaten
1¼ cups/300 ml buttermilk
½ cup/120 ml milk

❶ Preheat the oven to 425° F/220° C/ Gas 7. Mix the flour, baking powder, salt, sugar, and chocolate chips in a large bowl.

❷ Melt the butter and chocolate together in a bowl over a pan of gently simmering water, then leave to cool. Whisk in the eggs, buttermilk, and milk. Pour into the dry ingredients and mix quickly.

❸ Drop tablespoons of the mixture into muffin cases in a muffin pan. Cook 20 minutes until risen and firm to the touch.

❹ To serve, drizzle with melted chocolate, if desired.

Level sponge cakes

Fill cake pans about two-thirds full and spread the batter well into the corners and sides. Leave a slight hollow in the center and set in the preheated oven. The cake is done when it shrinks from the sides of the pan and springs back when lightly touched with the finger. After removing the cake from the oven, leave to cool in the tin for 5 minutes. Loosen the sides and turn it out on a rack to finish the cooling process. Frost the cake only after it is thoroughly cool.

Cake decoration

A home-made piping bag can be made by rolling up a piece of wax paper into a cone shape so that one end forms a point. Snip off the point with scissors. Insert icing at the wide end and squeeze it out through the pointed end. To decorate a cake directly on its serving plate, slip strips of wax paper under the edge of the cake, allowing them to hang over the rim of the plate. Frost the cake, then, with a quick motion, pull out the paper. This leaves the serving plate clean and without a trace of frosting.

Creamed sponge cake

Serves 6–8

¾ cup/175 g butter
⅔ cup/150 g sugar
3 eggs

1 cup/120 g self-rising flour
jelly or whipped cream and soft fruit
   to fill

❶ Preheat the oven to 375° F/190° C/ Gas 5. Base-line two 7-inch/18-cm round sandwich pans with nonstick baking parchment.

❷ Whisk the butter and sugar with a hand-held electric mixer or a wooden spoon in a mixing bowl until they are pale and fluffy and no longer grainy.

❸ Break the eggs into a separate bowl. Using a balloon whisk, beat the eggs to break them up slightly. This makes them easier to add to the rest of the mixture.

❹ A little at a time, gradually beat the eggs into the butter and sugar

mixture. Make sure you whisk well after each addition of egg. If the mixture begins to curdle, add a small spoonful of the flour.

❺ Sift the flour over the mixture. Fold it into the mixture gently using a large metal spoon and a figure-of-eight movement until well combined.

❻ Spoon the mixture into the pans and bake until golden and the center of the cake springs back when pressed lightly, about 20–25 minutes. Turn out to cool on wire racks. Sandwich together with jelly or whipped cream and soft fruit when cold.

Layered cakes

To split a cake into two even layers, measure halfway up the side of the cake and insert wooden picks all around, about 1–1½ inches/3.5 cm apart. Rest a long serrated knife on the wooden picks, using them as a guide on where to slice. Alternately, loop a length of unflavored waxed dental floss around the outside of the cake at the point you want the cut, then cross the ends and pull gently but firmly. The floss will cut right through the cake.

Get fruity

When making fruit cake, plump up dried fruit by placing it in a shallow baking dish, sprinkling generously with water, covering, then placing the dish in the oven as it heats for baking the cake. In 10–15 minutes the fruit will be soft and plump. Cool slightly and add to the cake batter.

American sponge cake

Serves 6–8

3 large eggs, separated
½ cup/120 g sugar

⅓ cup/75 g all-purpose flour, sifted

① Preheat the oven to 350° F/180° C/ Gas 4. Line the base of an 8-inch/ 23-cm springform tube pan.

② Put the egg yolks into a large, roomy mixing bowl and add 4 tablespoons of the sugar. Whisk together using a hand-held electric mixer until the egg yolks are thick and pale yellow.

③ Remove the beaters and wash them in hot soapy water. In a separate, roomy bowl, and with the clean beaters, whisk the egg whites until they stand in stiff peaks.

④ Gradually whisk in the remaining sugar, sprinkling it over the surface 1 tablespoon at a time, making sure it is thoroughly incorporated before adding the next, until stiff and glossy.

⑤ Sift the flour over the egg yolks in the first bowl, then fold it in carefully using a spatula or large metal spoon.

⑥ Working quickly, immediately add the egg whites and fold them in with the spatula or spoon until thoroughly combined. Take care note to knock out the air in the mixture.

⑦ Spoon the mixture into the prepared pan and bake until golden and the top springs back when pressed lightly, 30–40 minutes.

⑧ Turn the pan upside down on a wire rack and let cool in the pan, 30 minutes. Run a knife around the inside of the pan then turn the cake out onto the rack. Turn right side up and let cool completely.

Using up the crumbs

Leftover cookies, store-bought or home-made, can be crumbled and stored in a sealed bag in the freezer. Use them for stuffing fruit or as the basis for the top of a fresh fruit cobbler.

Crisp cookies

Follow the same instruction in shopping for cookies as you do with cakes. Dry, crisp cookies should be stored separately from soft cookies to avoid them from becoming soft. Store them in a sealed tin with some sugar cubes or paper napkins to keep them crisp.

Choc-chip cookies

⅝ cup/150 g butter
¾ cup/150 g sugar
1 egg
½ tsp vanilla extract
1¾ cups/200 g plain flour

Makes 14

1 tsp baking powder
2 squares/50 g semisweet chocolate, chopped
2 squares/50 g white chocolate, chopped

❶ Preheat the oven to 350° F/180° C/gas 4. Lightly grease 2 or 3 baking trays.

❷ Beat together the butter and sugar until pale and fluffy. Beat in the egg and vanilla extract.

❸ Sift the flour and baking powder together and beat into the mixture. Stir in the semi-sweet and white chocolate until well combined.

❹ Place the rounded tablespoons of the mixture on the baking trays, leaving plenty of space around each one as the cookies will almost double in size.

❺ Bake for 12–15 minutes until golden. Allow to cool on the baking tray for 2–3 minutes, then transfer to a wire rack to cool completely. Store in an airtight container for up to 5 days.

Cookie party

A cookie decorating party is a fun activity to keep a group of kids occupied. Bake cookies in advance. Cover a worktable with a plastic disposable cover, lay out bowls of colored icings and various toppings and candies for decorations. The kids will take it from there and everyone goes home from the party with a souvenir.

Cookie gift

Add a fresh whole vanilla bean or cut and dried orange peel to a box of plain cookies you present as a gift. These added ingredients impart their flavor and aroma to the cookies.

bakery & dairy

Hot from the oven

It is much easier to handle and roll cookie dough if it is refrigerated first for 15–30 minutes. This prevents the dough from sticking even if it is soft. Soft dough may require more flour, but too much flour may make the cookies hard and brittle. Use a floured board for rolling and only as much dough as can be managed at one time. Flour the rolling pin lightly and roll out the dough to the desired thickness. Cut shapes as close together as possible and save all the trimmings for the final roll. Transfer the cut cookie dough to a pan or baking sheet and put in the upper third of the oven. Watch closely to avoid burnt edges.

For convenience sake

Frozen pastry and pie dough is available in most supermarkets. It is quick and easy to use for sweet or savory dishes—quiches, pies, and tarts. Pie dough, puff pastry, phyllo, and strudel pastries are examples of the pastries available ready made. Having bought pastry in the freezer is excellent for impromptu baking.

Pastry preparation

Chill the pastry dough before rolling, and afterwards before baking, to relax the gluten further. Submerge your knife in a glass of very hot water between slicing pieces of pastry to create a clean and uniform finish. Wipe the blade between slices as necessary. Brush beaten egg over the dough when it is formed in the mold or pan and freeze for 10 minutes. This helps seal the crust and is particularly helpful with wet fillings.

Fast defrost

Prepared pie dough can be rolled into a ball, double-wrapped in plastic, and stored in the freezer for up to 3 months. When preparing a crust, remove the dough from the freezer and leave at room temperature for 15 minutes. Grate the amount of dough you need onto a pie pan, press, and spread evenly with your fingers. The remaining ball of dough may be re-wrapped and returned to the freezer for storage. Pie dough may also be frozen in the pie pan or in flat, individually wrapped discs for immediate use and fast defrost time. Frozen dough has a tendency to become dry, so once it is formed in the pan, you may wish to brush the surface with melted butter.

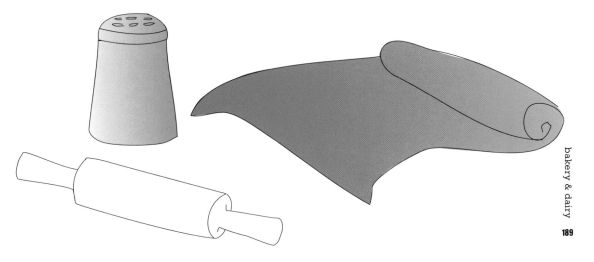

bakery & dairy

Apple pie

Serves 4–6

FOR THE CRUST
1½ cups/175 g all-purpose flour
½ tbsp salt
½ cup/100 g butter
about ¼ cup/60 ml iced water
egg white or cream, for glazing

FOR THE FILLING
6 cups/600 g peeled and cored tart
apples, thinly sliced

1 tbsp lemon juice
¾ cup/175 g sugar
¼ cup/60 g brown sugar
2 tbsp all-purpose flour
⅛ tbsp salt
¼ tbsp freshly grated nutmeg
¼ tbsp ground cinnamon
1 tbsp butter

❶ Preheat the oven to 450° F/230° C/ Gas 8.

❷ To make the crust, sift together the flour and salt. Blend the butter with the flour mixture by rubbing lightly together with the tips of your fingers until it resembles cornmeal in consistency. Work quickly to minimize the heat transferred from your fingers. Slowly mix in the water with a fork until the dough begins to clump together, then press it lightly into a ball. Wrap and chill for 1 hour.

❸ Remove the dough from the refrigerator and divide it in half. Dust a work surface and rolling pin lightly with flour. Flatten each ball of dough, sprinkle with flour, and roll it from the center out into a circle about 11 inches/27.5 cm in diameter. Lay the first circle over the bottom of a 10-inch/25-cm pie pan.

❹ Toss the apple slices in lemon juice to prevent them from turning brown and arrange them closely together in the lined pan. Mix the sugars, flour, salt, nutmeg, cinnamon and butter for the filling, and sprinkle over the apples.

❺ With a small cutter, cut out steam vents in the second circle of dough. Lay it loosely over the apples and fold the overhang under the rim of the pan to seal. Trim off excess dough. Press firmly around the rim with the tines of a fork. Glaze by brushing lightly with whisked egg white or cream.

❻ For a glistening, sugary top, sprinkle lightly with sugar. Bake for 10 minutes on the lowest shelf of the oven, then reduce the temperature to 350° F/180° C/Gas 4 and bake for 30–45 minutes more. To brown the crust, move the pie higher up in the oven for the last 10 minutes of baking. The apples are done when juice bubbles from the steam vents and the fruit feels tender when skewered. Place the pie on a wire rack and allow to cool for 3 hours. Serve warm with your favorite ice cream.

Perfect pies

A piecrust is easier to make when all the ingredients are cool. Place the lower crust in the pan so it covers the surface smoothly. Be sure no air lurks beneath the surface. This prevents the crust from pushing out of shape while baking. Fold the top crust over the lower crust before crimping the circumference edge. This will keep the juices in the pie.

Soggy pies

Custard-type pies should be baked at a high temperature for about 10 minutes to avoid a soggy crust. Prevent soggy piecrusts by sprinkling confectioners' sugar on them before adding the filling. If a pie filling calls for cornstarch, never boil it for more than 3 minutes. This will help to prevent the filling from becoming too thin.

Pizza dough

1 oz/25 g fresh yeast
1 tbsp superfine sugar
2 cups/500 ml tepid water

Serves 4

8 cups/900 g all-purpose flour
1½oz/ 40 g coarse sea salt
cornmeal, for dusting

1 Mix the yeast with the sugar, and half the water until it has completely dissolved.

2 Mix the flour and salt together and pour into a mound on a large clean surface. Create a well in the center of the mound and pour the yeast liquid into the well. With one hand, gradually mix the flour into the liquid to make a thick batter in the middle of the well. Add the remaining water and knead in the rest of the flour to form a moist dough.

3 Knead the dough thoroughly by pressing, folding, rolling, and pushing it. Keep the soft dough moving to prevent it from sticking and sprinkle a little flour on the surface occasionally if necessary. Knead until the dough is smooth and very elastic.

4 Place in a floured bowl, cover with plastic wrap, and leave in a warm place for about 1 hour. The dough should virtually double in size.

5 Preheat the oven to 475° F/240° C/ Gas 9. Preheat pizza stones or heavy baking sheets on the highest shelf.

6 Divide the dough into quarters and roll into ball shapes. Flatten each ball with a rolling pin or your hands (dusted with flour) and stretch into the shape you desire. Each pizza dough should have a even ½ inch/ 1 cm thickness. Sprinkle a clean working surface with a little cornmeal. This adds flavor and texture to the bottom of the finished crust. Lay the dough on top, one at a time, then place onto the preheated baking sheets or stone you will be using for the oven. Press the edge of the dough to form a ¾ inch/2 cm wide rim around the circumference to contain the topping.

7 Add the topping within the rim and bake for 7 minutes, or until the crust is golden brown color.

Croissants

Revitalize

Day-old croissants can be sprinkled with a little water before warming in the oven. This keeps the crust crispy and the inside moist. Cooked croissants may be frozen, and have a freezer life of about 3 months. Wrap them individually so that the required number can be removed.

Tortillas

As good as new

Leftover tortillas or those that have become dry in the refrigerator may be easily reconstituted. Use a mister and spray them with water until moist. Heat them in a lightly oiled pan or on a griddle until supple.

Batter

Freezing Batter

Pour pancake or waffle batter into a washed waxed milk carton, seal it, and freeze. When you are ready to use it, defrost the carton for 30 minutes. Take off the covering or slice through the container to remove the amount you wish to use. The remaining amount may be covered and placed back in the freezer.

Summer berry crêpes

Serves 4

FOR THE CRÊPES
scant 1 cup/100 g all-purpose flour
pinch salt
1 large egg
1 cup/300 ml milk
a few drops vanilla essence
4 tbsp water
1 tbsp/15 g butter
1 tbsp sunflower oil

FOR THE FRUIT
1 tbsp/15 g butter
4 tbsp sugar
1 tbsp grated orange peel
5 tbsp fresh orange juice
¼ lb/350 g mixed summer fruits, e.g.
   strawberries, raspberries, blue
   berries, black berries
2 tbsp Grand Marnier
1 tbsp confectioners' sugar
whipped cream to serve
fresh fruit or mint leaves, to
   decorate (optional)

❶ Sift the flour into a bowl with the salt and make a well in the center. Break in the egg and gradually add half the milk, whisking briskly to draw the flour into the egg.

❷ Whisk in the remaining milk, vanilla essence, and water to make a smooth batter with the consistency of light cream.

❸ Heat a small, nonstick skillet and add the butter and oil. When the butter has melted, pour into a small heatproof bowl and return the pan to the heat. Add a small ladleful of the batter and swirl it around the base of the pan until evenly coated. Cook until golden underneath, then flip the crêpe over and cook on the other side,

1–2 minutes in total. Slide the crêpe from the pan onto a plate. Repeat with the remaining batter, adding a little butter and oil mixture between crêpes.

❹ For the fruit, melt the butter in a saucepan, stir in the sugar, and cook gently for 1–2 minutes until golden brown. Add the orange peel and juice and swirl the pan until the sugar has dissolved. Add the fruit and Grand Marnier and cook until the fruit juices begin to run.

❺ Fold two crêpes onto each serving plate and top with a spoonful of the fruit. Serve with cream and decorate with fresh fruit or mint, if desired.

Dairy products

Milk

Buttermilk
This tangy, low-fat milk can be used instead of oil in salad dressings or in baking or milkshakes. As an alternative to buttermilk, add a splash of lemon juice to milk to create a similarly sour taste.

Cooking with milk
Milk burns very easily when heated, so use a heavy-based pan over a medium heat, stirring all the time.

Cold comfort
Select milk at the end of your shopping trip so that it will still be cold when you put it into your refrigerator at home.

Breast milk
Following the birth of a baby, breast milk production is increased by usage. Extra milk can be frozen in specially made sanitized sealed bags in the freezer. This is useful as fast food when the mother is away for limited periods of time.

Chocolate milkshake

Makes 2 large shakes

**2 cups/600 ml milk
5 scoops chocolate ice cream
2 tbsp drinking chocolate powder
2 tbsp ready-made
   chocolate sauce (optional)**

❶ Place the milk, ice cream, and drinking chocolate in a liquidizer and blend until thick and frothy.

❷ Pour the drink into two tall glasses; stir in a tablespoon of your favorite chocolate sauce, if using.

bakery & dairy

Cool cream

Cream should be stored in the refrigerator. Make sure that the container is opaque in order to preserve the vitamin B content of the cream. Unopened pasteurized cream may be refrigerated for up to 5 days. Before the expiration date, leftover cream may be poured into an ice-cube tray and stored in the freezer for up to 3 months. The cubes may be used in sauces, but not for whipped cream.

Iced cream

Place dollops of sweetened or flavored whipping cream on a waxed paper-lined baking pan in the freezer. Use it as a topping for piping hot coffee drinks.

Cream for whipping

Cream that has no less than 40 percent fat will render the richest whipping cream. By chilling the bowl of cream with the beater or whisk in the refrigerator, the cream will whip up to produce more volume. This method is particularly helpful in warm weather.

Flavored cream

Add powdered sugar to whipping cream for added sweetness and maintenance of shape. Consider using liqueurs and oil essences during the whipping process for additional flavor. Make flavored rosettes of whipping cream by adding combinations of cinnamon, cocoa, finely chopped nuts, and citrus zest. Pipe them onto a foil-lined baking sheet and freeze. Once they are frozen, store them in a self-sealing plastic bag. When you are ready to serve dessert, remove them from the freezer, place a rosette on each serving, and allow 10 minutes for them to thaw.

Keeping it fresh

Hard cheeses, like Parmesan, can be wrapped in a cloth dampened with salt water, beer, or vinegar, then set in a sealed plastic box in the refrigerator to keep from turning hard. Grated cheese can be stored with a sugar cube to absorb excess moisture. To prevent dryness in firm cheeses, such as Cheddar or Swiss, spread a little butter over the cut surfaces and cover in plastic wrap. Goat cheese placed in a small non-metallic bowl and covered with olive oil and plastic wrap will keep longer in the refrigerator.

Cooking with cheese

Cooking should be done at a low temperature so the cheese does not become tough or stringy. Some cheeses blend more easily than others. Cream cheese combines very easily and is used in many main dishes and desserts. To speed up the melting and blending of firmer cheeses, grate, slice, or shave them thinly before you heat them. Whenever possible, mix cheese with a sauce before adding it to other ingredients.

Freezing it

Only freeze cheese if it has over 45 per cent fat, otherwise it will separate. Grated Parmesan and other hard cheeses are handy to have in the freezer for omelets and sauces. Store in a self-sealing plastic bag. If you plan on grating soft cheeses like mozzarella, first place them in the freezer for 20 minutes to firm it up.

Cheese curls

Use a swivel potato peeler to shave decorative curls of hard cheese for the top of marinated or grilled Caesar salad and Mediterranean-style salads, as well as to top pasta dishes with chunky sauces.

Don't throw it away

Take hard, dried-out cheese and grate it in the food processor. Store in a sealed container in the refrigerator and use it for cheese sauces and as a gratin for the top of casseroles. Don't throw away the rind from hard cheeses like Parmesan or Romano. Use them to enhance the flavors in meat, bean and vegetable soups. Remove the rind before serving.

Cutting cheeses

• Small goat's milk cheeses— cut in half

• Round or square soft cheeses— cut like a cake into triangles, do not cut across the wedge

• Small or large drum-shaped cheeses—cut into discs and then into wedges like a cake

bakery & dairy

Cheese fondue

Serves 4

1 garlic clove
1½ cups/350 ml medium-dry Riesling
or Gewürztraminer wine
6 cups/750 g grated hard cheese,
such as Gruyère or Emmental
1 tsp arrowroot
½ tsp Dijon mustard

⅓ cup/75 ml Kirshwasser or cherry
liqueur
2 tbsp salted butter
Pickled cornichons, pearl onions, and
baby beets, to serve
Crusty, day-old French bread, cut into
roughly 3-inch/8-cm square cubes

❶ First smash the clove of garlic with the flat side of a knife and rub the clove on the inside of the fondue pot.

❷ Pour the wine into the pot and heat on the stovetop to just below boiling for 5 minutes. Reduce the heat to low, add the cheese gradually, allowing each addition to melt before adding the next. Stir constantly with a wooden spoon.

❸ Mix the mustard and arrowroot to a paste, with the Kirshwasser. Gradually stir this into the fondue and continue stirring until the mixture thickens. Finally, melt the butter in the fondue.

❹ It is now ready for serving with a selection of pickled cornichons, pearl onions, and baby beets on the side. Skewer the bread with fondue forks and dip in.

Basic cheese sauce

Makes 2½ cups/600 ml

**2 cups/500 ml Basic white sauce
(page 54)**
**½ cup/60 g grated cheese, such as
cheddar, Gouda, or provolone**
1 tsp Dijon mustard
pinch of cayenne pepper
pinch of freshly grated nutmeg

❶ When the white sauce is boiling,
add the grated cheese, reduce the
heat, and stir until the cheese melts.

❷ Stir in the remaining ingredients.
Do not reboil the sauce. Use
immediately.

Icy cream

To avoid crusty discoloration on the surface of the ice cream once the container has been opened, lay a piece of parchment paper over the surface. As a general rule, home-made ice cream can be kept frozen for 1 month. Firm types should be allowed to soften in the refrigerator for 30 minutes before serving. Keeping the container in a sealed plastic bag will inhibit the absorption of other odors. Use an ice cream scoop dipped in warm water to serve.

Vanilla ice cream

Serves 8

2 cups/500 ml milk
8 egg yolks, beaten
scant ½ cup/100 g superfine sugar

1 cup/250 ml whipping cream
1 tsp vanilla extract

❶ Beat the egg yolks with the sugar until pale and thick.

❷ Heat the milk on the stovetop until it is just about to boil, taking care not to let the milk scorch.

❸ Pour the milk into the egg yolks. Strain the mixture through a fine sieve back into the saucepan, then gently heat, stirring continuously, until slightly thickened enough to coat the back of a wooden spoon.

❹ Take the pan off the heat. Stir, cover, and let stand to cool for 30 minutes.

❺ Whip the cream and vanilla until thick. Add the cream to the cooled custard mixture and fold it in lightly. Pour into a metal container with a tight-sealing lid, only filling up to a two-thirds capacity to allow for expansion. The metal conducts the cold faster.

❻ Freeze for 30 minutes, or until half frozen. Beat the mixture vigorously. Return to the freezer for at least 2 hours before serving.

Baking with yogurt

Try yogurt in baking recipes. Plain yogurt can often be used instead of milk, buttermilk, or sour cream in recipes for waffles, pancakes, and muffins.

Cooking with yogurt

Yogurt tends to separate when heated. To prevent this, add a little cornstarch before cooking and make sure you add it at the last minute to a dish, taking care not to let the yogurt boil.

Flavor enhancer
Add a pinch of salt to wake up the flavor in plain yogurt.

Tender yogurt

Yogurt is a very useful marinade for meat, adding flavor and acting as a tenderizer.

Butter

Safe storage

Store butter in a sealed container in the refrigerator because it can easily pick up the aroma and flavor of other foods. Fresh unsalted butter can be stored in the freezer for up to 6 months in a sealed container. Fresh salted butter can be stored in the freezer for up to 3 months in its original wrapper.

Grate stuff

If a recipe calls for butter and yours is hard, try grating it using the large holes of a box grater and holding the butter by the wrapper to prevent it from melting in the warmth of your hands.

Butter for creaming

To make butter easier to cream with sugar or flour, pop the amount of butter required into the microwave on medium-low power for a few seconds.

Clarifying butter

Many sautéed dishes call for clarified butter, which is good for frying as it can withstand higher temperatures than ordinary butter. You can make clarified butter by melting solid butter in a saucepan over very low heat. When it becomes liquid, three layers are created. Skim the froth off the top with a spoon. The middle layer represents the rich yellow butterfat. This is the clarified butter and should be slowly poured into a bowl. The milky sediment that remains on the bottom of the saucepan can be discarded. To save time, melt the butter in a self-sealing plastic bag.

Flavored butter

Mix a combination of a little wine, minced shallots, garlic, chives, and other fresh herbs thoroughly into softened butter. Refrigerate until hardened, then roll into a long tube. Cover with plastic wrap and place in the freezer. Slice into ¼ inch/5 mm slices to garnish a serving of grilled chops or steaks. This is a fast and easy addition of flavor to dishes that have no accompanying sauce.

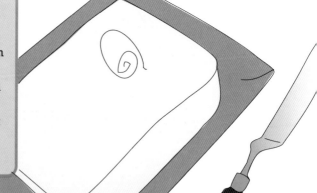

Sizing up eggs

Before buying, check the eggs in the carton for cracks or breakage. Gently jiggle each egg to make sure that none of them stick. Look at the date on the carton for the time of packing. Rarely are eggs available in the market within 48 hours of collection, thus the difference in taste between those refrigerated between 3 days and 2 weeks is minimally identifiable. The most commonly used egg is the hen egg and it is graded in quality and size by USDA standards. In descending order these are AA, A, B, and C, although the C grade refers to defective eggs not introduced into the consumer market. A standard size weight for an egg is around 2 oz/50 g. A large or jumbo egg is between 2½ and 3 oz/ 65–75 g.

Freezing

Whites and yolks should be frozen separately after stirring them and adding either a pinch of salt or sugar. Whites can be kept up to a year, and yolks for up to 6 months. Label and use salted eggs for savory dishes and sweet eggs for baking and desserts.

Poached eggs

Rapidly boil 4 cups/1 liter water in a saucepan for poaching eggs. Add 3 tablespoons white vinegar to help seal the whites. Crack up to 6 eggs open and drop the contents over the bubbles. The poaching should take about 4 minutes. You can test doneness by removing an egg with a slotted spoon. If the white is firm but the yolk portion is soft to the touch, it is done. Transfer the poached eggs to a bowl of warm water if they are being served hot, and to a bowl of cold water if their use is for salads.

Egg warming

When your recipe calls for room temperature egg whites, but they are still cold from the refrigerator, microwave them in an uncovered, heat-safe bowl. Heat no more than three at a time, with 30 percent heat, for 30 seconds.

bakery & dairy

Shaping meringues

• To make quenelles: Take two large metal spoons and scoop up some meringue with one of them. Scoop the mixture from the side of the spoon onto the other spoon. Repeat once or twice scraping the mixture from one spoon to the other, using the side not the front to make a smooth oval shape. Place on a baking sheet lined with waxed paper. Bake at 225° F/110° C/Gas ¼, 3–4 hours.

• To make fingers: Fit a piping bag with a large plain piping nozzle. Open out the top and stand in a tall jug. Spoon in the meringue and twist top to seal. Pipe into fingers on a baking sheet lined with waxed paper. Bake at 225° F/110° C/Gas ¼, 3–4 hours.

• To make nests: Spoon meringue into a piping bag fitted with a large star or plain nozzle. Open out top and stand in a tall jug. Spoon in meringue and seal top. Pipe 4-inch/ 10-cm circles in spirals onto a waxed paper-lined baking tray. Pipe more meringue around the edges of the circles to make "walls." Bake at 250° F/120°C/Gas ½, 1 hour.

Perfect meringues

Serves 4

4 egg whites | ⅔ **cup/150 g sugar**

❶ Whisk the egg whites to stiff peaks. Add half the sugar, 1 tablespoon at a time. Continue beating for 30 seconds. The meringue should be glossy and form short, soft peaks.

❷ Fold in the rest of the sugar with a large metal spoon, carefully and thoroughly. The meringue should now be able to hold long, stiff peaks when the whisk is lifted. Use as required.

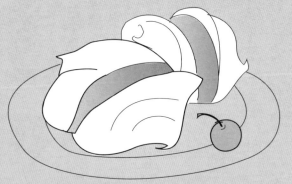

Egg test

Most refrigerators have their own compartment for eggs. Use it in order to prevent breakage and guard against the effects of fluctuations in temperature through opening and closing of the door. If you prefer to store them in the carton, make sure the container has a closing cover. This is to prevent the absorption of kitchen odors through their porous shells. It also helps prevent the loss of moisture. Eggs should always be stored with the pointed, or narrowest, side down.

This will keep the yolk in a suspended state. Eggs keep for approximately 3 weeks. To check whether they are fresh, try the following test. Dissolve 2 tablespoons of salt in 2 cups/500 ml of water. Place the unopened egg into the solution. If it sinks to the bottom, you may use it, if doesn't, it should not be eaten. If storing hard-boiled eggs in the refrigerator, mark them with a grease pencil to distinguish them from uncooked ones.

Scrambled eggs

Make your scrambled eggs creamier by adding 1 uncooked egg and 1 tablespoon soft butter to the pan before removing it from the heat.

Fresh check
Always break an egg into a bowl before adding any other ingredients. This is to ensure that it is fresh.

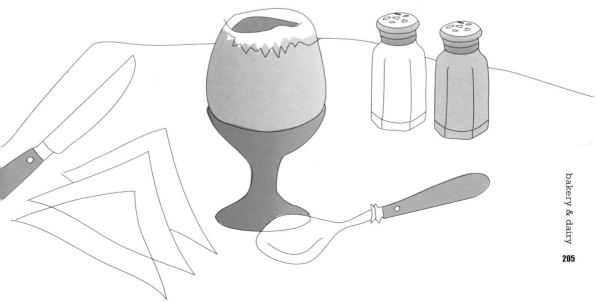

Egg whites

If you find it difficult to separate an egg white from its yolk, use a funnel. The white will run through and the yolk will be retained. Tip the yolk from the funnel into a small bowl. If you get a drop of yolk in the whites, remove with a cotton swab.

Before whisking the whites, make sure there is no trace of grease in the bowl or on the whisk, otherwise the whites will not become stiff. By adding a pinch of salt, the egg whites will stiffen faster, and by adding a few drops of lemon juice or sugar, they will maintain their firm shape. Always fold egg whites into a dish gradually, stirring as added.

Egg yolks

When adding egg yolks to a sauce that is being heated, remove some of the sauce first and stir it into the yolk, then add the mixture to the sauce.

Egg spinning

To check and see the extent to which an egg has boiled, spin it in water. An egg that is harder cooked, spins fast. A softer cooked egg spins slower. If the eggshell should crack during boiling, add salt or vinegar to seal it and prevent leakage of the content.

Batters

Crêpe, pancake, and waffle batters are best when they are covered and allowed to rest for 2 hours in the refrigerator before they are used in cooking, so the starch in the flour can absorb the water. The perfect batter should be the consistency of pouring cream.

Cheese soufflé

Serves 4

¼ cup/50 g butter, plus extra for greasing
⅓ cup/50 g all-purpose flour
1 cup/300 ml milk
5 eggs, separated

pinch of fresh grated nutmeg
¼ tsp English mustard powder
½ lb/225 g Cheddar cheese, grated
1 tbsp freshly grated Parmesan

❶ Preheat the oven to 180° C/350° F/ Gas 4. Grease a 5½ cup/1.5 liter soufflé dish with butter. Melt the butter in a large saucepan, add the flour, and cook for 1 minute. Whisk in the milk, then bring to the boil, stirring until thickened. Remove from the heat and add the nutmeg, mustard, and seasoning. Stir in the cheese and let cool a few minutes.

❷ Whisk in the egg yolks. Whisk the egg whites until stiff but not dry, beat in 1 tablespoon, then fold in the rest.

❸ Pour the mixture into the soufflé dish and run your finger around the top inside edge. Sprinkle with Parmesan and bake, 30–40 minutes.

Flat is best

Always break eggs on a flat surface, as the shell stays together in larger pieces. If you break eggs on the edge of bowls there is always the danger that small pieces of shell will fall in.

Room temperature

Always allow eggs to warm to room temperature before boiling as eggs used directly from the refrigerator are more likely to crack when boiled

Egg safety

Pregnant women, the sick, elderly, or infirm who are advised to avoid eating part-cooked or raw eggs should follow these simple rules:
• Buy from a reputable supplier with a good turnover always use within the suggested time.
• Store in the closed carton in the refrigerator.
• Avoid all recipes using raw egg.
• Buy pasteurized mayonnaise and

similar sauces instead of making them with raw egg.
• Always cook eggs until the white and yolk are both firm—avoid custards and similar "soft" cooked egg dishes.
• Look out for pasteurized eggs in the refrigerated dairy case if lightly cooked eggs are required, for example for scrambling.
• Scramble eggs until they are firm and creamy, not thin and soft.

easy
solutions

Emergency!

If flames should appear on the stovetop while pan or deep-fat frying, turn off the heat and cover the pan or pot with a lid immediately. Do not try to move the pan or pot. Do not attempt to extinguish the flames with water as this could exacerbate the fire and create an explosion. Make sure there is no standing water in the vicinity. Keep oven mitts handy for lifting pots away.

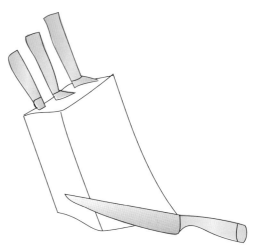

Knife safety

Always carry a knife with the point directed down towards the floor. Let a knife fall if you lose grip on it. It is often more dangerous to attempt to catch it. Keep your knives sharp. A dull blade can easily shift when cutting. Remember to wash knives separately from other items in a sink. Avoid the mistake of reaching into soapy water and cutting yourself needlessly.

Fire precautions

Prevent flare-ups of flame by choosing pans that cover the heat source entirely. Never fill the pan up more than two-thirds full when deep-fat frying. Hot fat explodes when it comes into contact with water. Make sure food is completely dry before frying. Clean up splatters of fat from the stove and sides of the pan as quickly as possible.

Splash-free fondue

When making a fondue with oil, put a little whole parsley into the pot to reduce the possibility of burning guests by splattering.

Ants, out!

Seal off entrance cracks with putty or petroleum jelly. Try sprinkling red pepper on floors and countertops to discourage pests. If you can, treat the nest with branded insect control spray. Most importantly, keep your kitchen clean!

Splatter-free frying

Sprinkle a little flour or salt into a pan before beginning to fry foods in oil. When frying foods in fat or ingredients with a high fat content, use a flat fine-mesh screen, similar to a strainer, over the top of the pan.

Opening bottles and jars

When glass bottles or jars are difficult to open, try one of the following methods. First, try donning a rubber glove and giving the top a twist. For jars with metal-based tops, run hot water over the top to expand the width of the lid. Dry it off with a cloth before turning it. A rap with the base of your palm to the bottom of the jar can also aid in the opening of a stubborn top. If the contents are in oil, rub oil between the container and lid. If the contents are alcohol or perfume, rub alcohol over the meeting point of the container and lid. Use a cloth to protect your hand and loosen the top.

Scalded milk
If your recipe calls for scalded milk, first rinse the pan with running cold water to make cleaning easier.

Faulty cans

Don't take any chances if you find that the seal of your can ruptures or pops up. The canned goods may have been overcooked in processing or stored improperly. Further evidence of that can be seen with bulging lids and surfaces, liquids with a murky appearance, mold, and discoloration. Discard immediately to avoid potential contamination and illness.

Successful meringues

Make sure that your egg whites are completely yolk free. Use a cotton swab to dab out any questionable trace.

Macho marinade

To thicken a marinade to ensure it adheres to fish, poultry, or meat, combine thoroughly with 1 teaspoon cornstarch.

Curdle-free yogurt

When introducing yogurt into a sauce, avoid curdling by combining the yogurt with 1 teaspoon cornstarch in a mixing bowl. Spoon in some of the hot sauce mixture and whisk vigorously. Then add the contents of the bowl to the pan of sauce. Stir until the sauce thickens.

Meringue perfection

Avoid shrinkage or falling of meringue on pies by spreading it completely over the top to the edges of the pan. No exposed under surface should be visible. It also helps when the meringue is topped onto a hot filling.

Prevent curdling cream

To prevent cream from curdling in a sauce, remove 1/2 cup/120 ml of the sauce and whisk in the amount of cream the recipe calls for. Turn off the heat and whisk in the sauce and cream mixture.

Egg damage

Cracked eggs should only be used in dishes that are thoroughly cooked. They may contain bacteria. If you don't know how long the egg has been cracked, don't take a chance by using it.

Milder garlic

Produce a milder taste in garlic by blanching whole, unpeeled cloves in boiling water for 3 minutes. This also loosens the outer skin and makes them a cinch to peel.

Dried herb revival

Revive the life in dried herbs before introducing them to uncooked dishes such as salads or dips. Bruise them with a mortar and pestle. Mix them in a small bowl with chopped onion or shallots and a little lemon juice. Add finely chopped flat-leaf parsley to create a fresher aroma and taste. Let rest for 15 minutes before using.

Canned taste

Some vegetables from the can may have an unpleasant metallic aroma and taste. Artichoke, bamboo shoots, hearts of palm, mushrooms, and water chestnuts are examples. Drain the vegetables and blanch for 1 minute in boiling water with 1 teaspoon lemon juice added. Rinse in cool water.

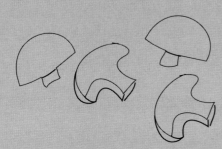

Make the most of mushrooms

Revive mushrooms that have become dry and tough by soaking them in a cup of sherry or red wine for 15 minutes. Bring this mixture to the boil and stir in a little heavy cream.

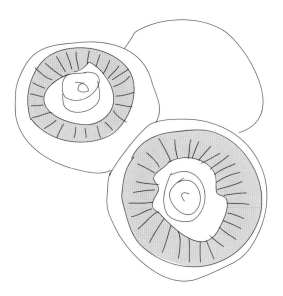

Gingerly does it

Fresh ginger is acidic. If your recipe calls for it mixed with a dairy milk product in a heated sauce, blanch it whole for 2 minutes in boiling water first. Cut or grate it depending on the recipe. This should prevent potential curdling.

Brown sugar gone hard

Soften brown sugar that has gone hard by placing it with a wedge of apple in a heat-resistant covered dish. Set your microwave to the maximum temperature and heat for 30 seconds. Remove the apple.

To ripen bananas

Soften unripened bananas for baking by piercing them in four locations with a skewer. The skins should be left on. Microwave on an uncovered plate at maximum temperature for 30 seconds. Flip them over and zap for another 30 seconds. Cool down, peel, mash, and use in your favorite banana bread recipe.

Be proactive

If recipes go awry, there are often ways to correct them before it is too late. Be proactive at all times and try to prevent problems before they happen. Even if it's too late and you've had a culinary disaster, there's usually a way to make something better and avoid waste.

Too hot chile

Grated dark bitter chocolate will add body to a thin chile stew. It also helps to integrate flavors and mellow the intensity of heat. Begin by adding 1 tablespoon chocolate, and repeat every 10 minutes depending on the quantity of chile, using up to 4 tablespoons.

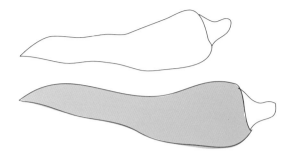

Baking powder, is it still effective?

Test its effectiveness before you use it. If a pinch thrown into a cup of warm water begins to foam, it is still good. Never extract the powder from the container with a wet measuring spoon. Contact with water could destroy the entire contents of the tin.

Cake pick-me-up

Dense cakes and fruit breads can be reconstituted from dryness or overbaking by soaking them momentarily in milk and placing them in a warm oven for a few minutes. An alternative is soaking the cake in sherry, rum, or brandy as a dessert, or making a simple syrup spiked with your favorite liqueur. Top it off with fresh berries, chopped nuts, or whipping cream.

To slow the dough

Refrigerate bread dough if you are interrupted during making and have to leave. The more gradual process can actually enhance the flavor and texture of the bread.

Watery creamed butter

Creamed butter for baking should have a light and fluffy consistency. If for some reason it becomes watery or thin, cool it down in the refrigerator right away. Resume beating after it has become firm.

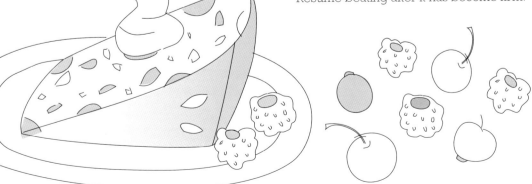

Overwhipped cream

If your cream is overwhipped, gradually fold in 2 to 3 tablespoons of unwhipped milk or cream to the mixture, taking care not to stir too hard.

Fruit salad too sweet?

If your fruit salad tastes too sweet and you'd like to give it a little kick, consider adding some freshly grated ginger or freshly squeezed lemon juice.

Salty gravy or soup?

Don't despair if you've oversalted. Keep instant mashed potatoes on hand and stir some in to repair the damage. Add a little more liquid to offset the thickening. If you find that your soup is too salty, you can add 1 to 2 peeled potatoes to the liquid. This will help to absorb some of the salt content. Remove the potatoes when they are cooked through so as not to thicken the liquid.

Overwhipped egg whites

If you have overwhipped egg whites, beat a new one separately until it is just frothy. Fold that into the mixture and whip again to the desired consistency.

Perfect hollandaise

If the sauce has broken, smooth it out by adding 2 tablespoons boiling water and whisk vigorously.

Magic mash

In the event that mashed potatoes become gluey, grainy, or overcooked, don't despair. Beat an egg white until stiff and fold gently into the mash. Add seasonings or ingredients like ground nutmeg, snipped chives, bacon bits, grated cheese, salt and pepper. Spread onto a lightly greased baking dish and bake until a golden brown finish is rendered. If your mashed potatoes simply lack character, consider adding some garlic purée or freshly grated horseradish to give the flavor a boost.

Undercooked chicken

If you discover that the chicken breast you thought was cooked through is in fact pink inside, slice it in half lengthwise and sauté it in a little hot oil or melted butter to cook it through. Alternatively, wrap it in aluminum foil and bake for 10 minutes at 350° F/180° C/Gas 4.

Vegetables too salty?

Pour boiling water over vegetables that have been oversalted. Drain thoroughly. If they still taste too salty, toss with a little warm cream.

Greasy soup

A leaf of lettuce added to a pot of soup will absorb excess fat from the top. Remove and discard the lettuce once the job is done. An alternative approach is to dredge a piece of soft bread across the surface of the liquid to remove the majority of grease.

Overcooked vegetables

Peas, beans, and root vegetable that have overcooked can be rescued by preparing them as a purée. Blend them in a food processor and stir in a little heavy cream when you heat them up.

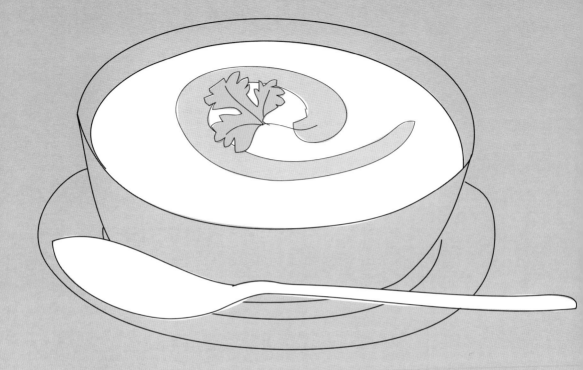

Thin sauce

If you find that your sauce is too thin, don't panic. Add some powdered arrowroot—it is tasteless and not starchy, and will mix easily into a sauce without making it lumpy. Add 1 teaspoon to the sauce and stir in. Alternatively, remove about ½ cup/120 ml of the sauce and whisk in 1 teaspoon cornstarch. Stir until completely dissolved, then reintroduce this mixture back into the sauce, stirring it in.

Adding yogurt

To prevent yogurt from curdling when adding it to stocks, soups, and sauces, blend a small amount of cornstarch with the yogurt. Next, whisk some of the hot stock into the yogurt and then add the whole mixture to the stock and cook. Stir the stock until it has thickened.

From broth to soup

A fast way to thicken your soup is with a potato. Stab it multiple times with the tines of a fork. Wrap it in a paper towel and place in the microwave at maximum heat for 6 minutes. When the potato is soft, remove the skin with your fingers and a fork. Mash or press through a potato ricer directly into the soup and stir.

Too lumpy

If you find that your sauce or gravy is lumpy, just strain it through a sieve. You could also beat the lumpy gravy with a whisk until smooth and then reheat, stirring constantly. To mask the taste of burnt gravy, stir in a teaspoon of peanut butter.

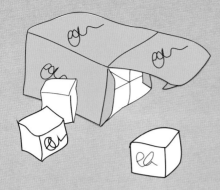

Cloudy stock

Through prolonged boiling, stock can become cloudy. When this happens, clarify with 1 to 2 whisked egg whites. Add to the liquid as it comes to the boil and simmer for 10 minutes. The impurities should float up to the foam. Strain the liquid through a sieve and repeat the process if necessary.

Garlic breath

Eat fresh parsley or chew on a whole fresh coffee bean to get rid of the pungent aroma of garlic or onion.

Garlic fingers

If you are chopping raw garlic or rubbing it into meat, no doubt the odor will linger on your hands. Rub the bottom of a stainless steel spoon over your hands and fingertips while they are submerged under warm running water. Follow this by washing them in soapy warm water. The smell will vanish.

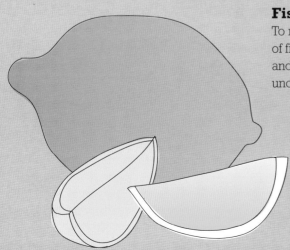

Fishy fingers

To rid your fingers of the lingering smell of fish, rub salt and lemon juice over them and work in vigorously. Rinse your hands under cold running water.

index

acorn squash 139
aluminum foil 31
aluminum kitchenware 24
   cleaning 36
American sponge cake
   186
anchovies 70
ants 210
apples 98
   apple pie 190
   apple sauce 98
apricots in liqueur 107
artichokes 123
asparagus 124–5
avocado 113–14

baby vegetables 124–5
bacon 154
bagels 178, 179
bakery 178–94
baking powder 215
Balsamic vinegar 68
bamboo steamers,
   cleaning 40
bananas 99
   ripening 214
barbecuing fish 169
barley 57
basic cheese sauce 199
basil 119, 120, 121
batter 193, 206
bay leaves 120
beans
   dried 57–9, 134
   fresh 133
beef 149–52
   beef and wine casserole
   149
beefburgers 150, 151
beets 119
berries 105–6
blanching food 86–7
blenders, cleaning 41
blueberries 105
boiled eggs 206
boiling 86
   fish 168

Bolognese shells 60
bottles, opening 211
bouquet garni 120
bread 178–83, 215
bread and butter pudding
   181
bread crumbs 178
bread pans 26
breadcrumb batter 166
breast milk 195
brick floors, cleaning 43
broccoli 126
broiled lobster tails 174
broiling 91
   meat 148
brown rice 61
brown sugar 56, 214
Brussels sprouts 127
Brussels sprouts in pecan
   sauce 127
budget, kitchen planning
   10
bulghur wheat 57
burgers 150, 151
burnt-on food, cleaning
   36
butter 215
buttermilk 195, 202
butternut squash 139

cabbage 128
cake pans 26
cakes 183–6, 215
canned asparagus 125
cans 213
   faulty 211
caramel sauce 56
carrots 125
carving turkey 160
casseroles 148
   beef and wine casserole
   149
cast iron kitchenware 24
   cleaning 37
cauliflower 127
celery 117
champagne 77–8

cheese 197–9
   cheese fondue 198
   cheese sauce 199
   cheese soufflé 207
   Welsh rarebit 179
chervil 119, 120
chicken 158–9
   chicken rotisserie 93
   chicken stock 159
   undercooked 217
chiffonade, food
   preparation 83
chilies 57, 137, 215
   chili mango salsa 109
   chili oil 66
chives 120
choc-chip cookies 187
chocolate 74–5
   chocolate cakes 184
   chocolate chip muffins
   183
   chocolate milkshake 195
chopping, food
   preparation 82
chopping boards 15, 29
   cleaning 40
chopsticks 28
chores, sharing 34
chunky guacamole 114
cilantro 119, 120, 121
citrus fruits 102–4
clarifying butter 202
classic champagne
   cocktail 79
clay quarry tiles 12
cleaning 10, 12, 15,
   34–47
   cutting boards 20
   microwaves 22
   ovens 20
   shelves 16
club sandwiches 182
coffee 77
coffee and maple syrup
   frosting 77
coffee makers, cleaning
   40

color, in the kitchen 10
composting 46
confetti, food preparation
   82
cookers 19–21
   cleaning 45, 46
   cooking 85
cookies 186–8
   choc-chip cookies 187
copper kitchenware 24
   cleaning 37
corn 142
crab 175
cream 196, 212
   overwhipped 216
creamed sponge cake 184
croissants 193
croutons 180
crystal decanters, cleaning
   41
cucumber 118
cupboards 15
   stocking the 50–79
curries
   lamb and chickpea curry
   156
curtains, cleaning 44
cutlery cleanliness 47
cutting boards 15, 29
   cleaning 40

dairy products 195–207
dates 110
deep-frying 89
   safety 210
defrosting the fridge/
   freezer 18, 38
deodorizing the fridge 18
descaling fish 166
dicing 82
   meat 148
dill 119, 121
dimmer switches, lighting
   17
discoloration, preventing
   84
dishwashers, cleaning 38

draining food 86
dried beans 57–9
dried chiles 137
dried fruits 110
dried mushrooms 141
dry-salting 95
duck 162–3
  duck a l'orange 163

earthenware 34
economical shopping 51
eggplants 138
eggs 203–7, 213
  overwhipped egg whites
    216
electric broiling 91
electric grinders 40
electrical deep-fat fryers
    89
electronic scales 30
endives 117
energy conservation 18
extraction fans and hoods
    20
  cleaning 39

fabric stains 46
fan assisted ovens 20
fat, duck and goose 162
fennel 121
figs 110
filleting fish 166
filleting knives 27
fires 210
fish 164–70, 219
  marinating 94
  poaching 87
  steaming 88
fish slices 30
fish stock 168
flan dishes 26
flavored butter 202
flavored cream 196
flooring 12
  cleaning 43
flour 54–5
flowers, edible 121
fondues 210

cheese fondue 198
food mixers and
    processors 22–3
freestanding appliances,
    gaps between 19
freezers 18
  see also frozen food
  cleaning 38, 45
  storing food 53
French onion soup 129
fresh beans 133
fresh herbs 15
fridge/freezer 18
  cleaning 38, 45
  storing food 53
frozen food 50, 51, 53
  bread 178, 179, 180
  cakes 184
  cheese 197
  chiles 137
  chocolate 74–5
  eggs 202
  fish and shellfish 165,
    173, 174, 175
  fruit 99, 100, 105
  meat 146
  mushrooms 141
  nuts and seeds 65
  pastry 189
  poultry 158
  stock ice cubes 68
  vegetables 59, 70, 111,
    128, 129, 133, 134,
    136, 139, 140
fruit 98–144
  canned 147
  dicing 82
  poaching 87
fruit cakes 184, 186
fruit salad 216
Fruity BBQ sauce 68
frying 89
  fish 168
  safety 210

garbage disposal 46
garlic 142–3, 213, 219
  roasted garlic 143

garnish, tomato 113
ginger 142, 214
glass cookware 25
glass shelves 15
glass windows, cleaning
    44
glasses, separating 35
glazed tiles 12
globe artichokes 123
gloves, protective 35
"golden triangle" 11
grains 57
grapes 100
graters 28
  grating ginger 142
gravy 160
  oversalting 216
green peppers 135
grilling 20
  fish 168
ground beef 150

ham 153
ham stock 153
hand blenders 22
hand held mixers 23
hanger steak 152
hardwood flooring 12
  cleaning 43
harvest apple sauce 98
hazelnuts, skinning 65
herbs 64, 119–22
  chopping 27, 82
  mortar and pestle 29
  reviving dried herbs
    213
  in salads 116
hollandaise sauce 216
homemade beefburgers
    151
homemade mayonnaise
    169
homemade tartare sauce
    168
homemade tomato purée
    70
honey 76
honeydew melons 101

hot chocolate sauce 75
hulls, berries 105

ice cream 200
ice cream scoops 30
ice cream shells, citrus
    fruits 103
Iced herb tea 64
irons, cleaning 38

jams, sterilizing jars 35
jars
  cleaning 46
  opening 211
  sterilizing 35
Jerusalem artichokes 123
juice
  citrus fruits 103
  fruit and vegetable 111
julienne, food preparation
    83

ketchup 71
kitchen tools 28–30
kitchenware 24–6
kiwi fruit 108
knives 27
  cleaning 40
  safety 210

labelling food 18
ladles 30
lamb 156–7
lamb and chickpea curry
    156
layered cakes 186
leeks 130
leftover ideas 134
lemonade 102
lemons 102–3, 123
lentils 59
lettuce 115
lighting 17
limes 102–3
  lime shrimp 172
linoleum 12
  cleaning 43
list making 50

liver 147
lobster 174
long-grain rice 61

Mâche 115
maize 57
mangoes 109
marinating 94, 212
  fish 169
  meat 147
  peppers 136
marjoram 120
mashed potatoes 132,
  217
mayonnaise, homemade
  169
measuring cups and jugs
  28
meat 146–57
meat tenderizing 84
melon ballers 30
melons 101
meringues 204, 212
Mexican refried beans
  58
mezzaluna 27, 82
microwaves 22
  cleaning 38
  cooking 85
milk 195
mineral water 79
mint 119
"mise en place" 82
mixers, food 22–3
mixing bowls 26
mortar and pestle 29
mushrooms 141
  reviving 214
mustard 72

nectarines 107
needle nose pliers 30
nonstick kitchenware 25,
  34
nuts and seeds 65

oatmeal 57
oils 66

olives 72
  olive foccacia 73
onions 129–30
oranges 103, 104
  duck a l'orange 163
  orange terrine 104
oregano 120
organization 34
  preparing food 82
  when shopping 51
ovens 19–21
  cleaning 45, 46
  cooking 85
oysters 171

packing, shopping 52
pan-fried salmon 170
pancake batter 193
paper plates 82
parchment paper 31
paring knives 27
parsley 119, 120, 121
parties, cleaning up 45
pasta 59–60
  cooking 87
pasta forks 30
pastry and pie dough
  189–92
pastry brushes 30
pea and bacon soup 135
peaches 107
pears 100
peas 134–5
peeling
  apples 98
  citrus fruits 103
  kiwi fruit 108
  tomatoes 111
peppers 135–6
pesto 122
pickles 70
  sterilizing jars 35
pies 189–92
pineapple 108
pizza dough 192
planning ahead 50
planning your kitchen
  10–15

plantains 99
plastic wrap 31
plums 107
poached eggs 203
poaching 87
  pears 100
pomegranates 109
pork 153–5
potatoes 131–2, 217
pots and pans
  cleaning 36–7
  heat-resistant tiles 15
  storage 16
pouch cooking 95
poultry 158–63
preparing and cooking
  food 82–95
preserves, sterilizing jars
  35
processors, food 22–3
protective gloves 35
prunes 110

raisins 110
raspberries 105
raspberry purée 105
recessed lighting 17
recycling 46
  recycled containers 31
red peppers 135
red wine 78
refrigerators see fridge/
  freezer
revolving shelves 17
ribbons, food preparation
  83
rice 61–2
risotto rice 61
roasting 92, 148
  duck 162
  potatoes 131
  roast beef 92
  roast peppers 136
  roasted eggplant purée
  138
  roasted garlic 143
  turkey 160
roasting bags 31

roasting pans 25
roller blinds, cleaning 44
rolling pins, cleaning 40
rosemary 120
rubbish bins, cleaning 47
rust stains, removing 37

sage 120
salad dressing 118
salads 115–16, 118
salmon 168
  pan-fried salmon 170
  salmon in a pouch 95
salsas
  chili mango salsa 109
salt 57, 67
salting meat 147
sandwich making tips 182
sauces
  basic cheese sauce 199
  Brussels sprouts in
    pecan sauce 127
  caramel sauce 56
  Fruity BBQ sauce 68
  harvest apple sauce 98
  hollandaise sauce 216
  homemade mayonnaise
    169
  homemade tartare sauce
    168
  hot chocolate sauce 75
  for red meat 148
  soy sauce 67–8
  tomato sauce for pasta
    112
  too thin 218
  white sauce 54
sausages 153
sautéing 90
scalded milk 211
scales 30
scissors 28
scrambled eggs 205
seasonal products 51
seeds 65
separating eggs 206
serrated knives 27
shellfish 171–5

shelving 15
  cleaning 16
  glass 15
  revolving 17
shopping 50, 51–2
short-grain rice 61
shrimps 172–3
  lime shrimp 172
silver, cleaning 40
sinks 13
  cleaning 39, 45
slate tiles, cleaning 43
slatted blinds, cleaning
  44
slicing, food preparation
  84
smoothie 23
snipping, dried fruits 110
snow peas 134
soufflés
  cheese soufflé 207
soups
  excess fat 217
  French onion soup 129
  oversalting 216
  pea and bacon soup
   135
  thickening 218
southern-fried chicken
  159
soy sauce 67–8
space, maximising 16
spaghetti squash 139
spices 63
spinach 126
spring vegetable risotto
  62
squash 139
squid 173
stainless steel kitchenware
  25
  cleaning 36
steaks, beef 152
steaming vegetables 88
steel kitchenware 24
sterilizing jars 35
stir-frying 91
stock 68–9

chicken stock 159
  cloudy 219
  fish stock 168
  ham stock 153
  vegetable stock 69
stock-boiled cabbage
  128
stocking the cupboards
  50–79
stone tiles 12
  cleaning 43
storage solutions 16–17
  containers and bags 31,
   41
store cupboard essentials
  54–79
stoves 19–21
  cleaning 45, 46
  cooking 85
strawberries 105
stuffed cabbage 128
stuffing 180
sugar 56, 214
summer berry crêpes 194
sweating vegetables 90

t*angy barbecue pork* 155
tarragon 119, 120
tartare sauce, homemade
  168
teflon, cleaning 37
telephones 34
tempura vegetables 90
tenderizing meat 84
thermometers 29
thyme 120
tiles
  floor 12, 43
  wall 10
time-savers, cleaning
  35
toasted nuts 65
toasterbags 180
toasters 179
  cleaning 40
tomato ketchup 71
tomato purée 70
tomatoes 111–13

homemade tomato purée
  70
tomato sauce for pasta
  112
tongs 30
tortillas 193
traffic flow, in the kitchen
  11
trash bins, cleaning 47
tuna 168
turkey 160–61

utensils 28–30
  storage 16

vanilla beans 75
vanilla ice cream 200
veal 157
vegetable stock 69
vegetables 115–43
  chopping 82
  dicing 82
  overcooked 217
  oversalting 217
  Spring vegetable risotto
   62
  vegetable stock 69
Venetian blinds, cleaning
  44
ventilation hoods 20
  cleaning 39
vinegar 68
vinyl flooring, cleaning
  43

waffle batter 193
water, mineral 79
watermelons 101
Welsh rarebit 179
wheat 57
whipping cream 196
white loaf 55
white rice 61, 62
white sauce 54
white sugar 56
white wine 78
window boxes 15
windows, cleaning 44

wine 78–9
wooden bowls 26
wooden utensils 28
work surfaces 15
  cleaning 47
working paths 11

yeast 56
yellow peppers 135
yogurt 201, 212
  curdling 218

zest, citrus fruits 102,
  103
zucchini 140

Special thanks to:

James Bannon, Rosemary Barron, Henrietta Bennett,

Joanne Bennett, Brigot Biraud, Misty Boopurrs,

Fritz Braker, Brooke Bremner, Kathleen Boswell

Brown, Eva Cassirer, Lady Elaine Chambers,

Cookie Childs, Barbara Jo Davis, Diana Donovan,

Fafar Faridjoo, Marc Ellen Teeter Garth, Alexander,

Ida and Olga Givot, Guido Givotelli, Joo and Weiner

Homi, Roz Howell, Bridget Jones, Jenny Mae Hughes,

Kafuka, Linda Kang, Alix Landfield, Bernice

Langsner, Sien Lemke, Princess Kate Maple, Mad Dog

Mateer, Hanne Paaske, Priscilla Pierce, Bimbo

Reynolds, JP Samuelson, Sandy Sanderson,

Timothy Schneider, Mette Tharaldsen, Jupp Thoennes,

Miss Tiny, and Bunny Wehrlin.